MOVE!

When God's Deliverance Requires
Man's Obedience.
31 Devotions

Amy Rogers

xulon
PRESS

MOVE!
When God's Deliverance Requires Man's Obedience 31 Devotions
by Amy Rogers

Printed in the United States of America.

ISBN 9781498492454

www.xulonpress.com

Table of Contents

To my husband, Scotty,
Thank you for allowing sin and failure to lead you to the Cross of Jesus Christ. Your pursuit of Him daily has given me the courage to seek His way no matter the cost. Our story isn't pretty, but your humility has allowed God (in Christ) to make it beautiful. Therefore, I'm honored to share our testimony and grateful to journey this life with you.

I love you,
Amy

Introduction

Trust in the Lord with all your heart, and do not lean on your own understanding. In all your ways acknowledge Him, and He will make your paths straight (New American Standard, Proverbs 3:5–6).

The past five years have been *interesting.* That's a great word, right? It covers all: heartbreak, sorrow, red-faced anger, relief, joy, and much, *much* more. I've experienced it all. And, through the "all," God has taught me a great deal about Himself.

The neat and tidy life I was living prior to my husband's adultery confession crashed in August of 2011. Life changed immediately. Not only was our family's foundation rocked to the core, our financial situation became scary. Job loss was imminent. Scotty could not continue as *Minister* to children and families in our church after confessing adultery. So, within a three day period, every security I'd known was gone.

Well, *almost* every!

The purity of our marriage was gone. Believe it or not, I had to grieve the loss of that purity like a death. After adultery, a lot can be restored through the power of God, but the innocence is gone and can't be recovered. To this day, that is the heaviest loss.

We lost a career, a church family, many friends, and the reputation we'd had in our community. Within a short time period, nearly everyone in our very small town heard our story or a twisted version of it. I'd never lived on that side of the stares, the looks of pity, or the whispers. For the most part, our community rallied around us. We felt it, and we were (and still are) grateful for such support. However, our pride took a hit, and relationships were forever changed.

We lost the certainty of anything familiar. Suddenly, Scotty was looking for a new job, we put a "for sale" sign in our yard, and we weren't sure about one thing beyond each individual day. We were established in a community that we loved just a few days before. Our children were in a school district I was confident would provide a great education all the way to college. We were content and had not even considered changing our circumstances. An earth-shattering confession brought uncertainty in all of these areas and more.

One thing did *not* change. One Person was more constant than I'd ever known Him to be. The Lord, my God, was present. When all else was crumbling, He was providing an unshakeable foundation. It was REAL! It was FELT! And, I couldn't keep quiet about it. Everything in me and around me said,

This is too much!
You can't handle it!
It's only going to get worse.

However, God's Word spoke louder than all of it. In the earliest moments of our life's shift, I came to know the grace that Paul described to the Corinthians as *sufficient.* The fact that I was still standing in the wake of such trauma was nothing short of a miracle. Still having hope in the midst of a seemingly hopeless situation was pure grace, but it was enough!

I began to write posts to our family's blog about God, His teachings, and all that HE was showing me (through our mess) about His character. At first, it felt really strange to be writing openly about my husband's adultery and our dealing with it. I knew it would make people uncomfortable. Adultery is a sin that couples and families spend their whole lives trying to hide. If ours hadn't been so public from the start, I'm sure hiding would have been my choice, too. Our story was public record, however, and I wanted God's work in our chaos to be equally as public.

I wrote and, *shockingly,* people read. Then notes, messages, texts, and comments began to make their way to me. God was speaking to others through my story. He was transforming hearts and opening eyes using my words. The truths He was teaching me in the middle of our big, giant mess seemed to be truths others needed to hear as well.

I've been sharing via that family blog for almost five years now. I LOVE it! Somewhere in that time frame people began encouraging me to write a book.

I CAN'T!

There's NO way!

I don't even know WHERE I'd start.

I've been waiting for a glimpse of that beginning. If I was *supposed* to write, I felt God would make the path leading to a book very obvious. This morning, God took me to the book of Joshua. Deuteronomy has been a favorite of mine for several years. I wanted to begin a study just beyond Moses and God's promise to Joshua and the fulfillment of His promise. I'm positive I've read it before, but Joshua 3:13 stopped me in my tracks:

> *And, it shall come about when the soles of the feet of the priests who carry the ark of the Lord, the Lord of all the earth, shall rest in the waters of the Jordan, the waters of the Jordan shall be cut off, and the waters which are flowing down from above shall stand in one heap.*

Do you see it? Can you tell what jerked me to a halt?

Possibly, it wasn't Joshua's words alone that caused the sudden "flag" in my spirit. Notice the difference in God's words to Moses from Exodus 14:16:

> *And as for you, lift up your staff and stretch out your hand over the sea and divide it, and the sons of Israel shall go through the midst of the sea on dry land.*

When God brought His people out of Egypt, He had Moses clear the water *before* they stepped in to cross it. I believe that was God's grace. They were scared and uncertain. God cleared the path prior to asking them to step into it.

In Joshua, though, God's people were spiritually stronger. They'd wandered in the desert for forty years. God had taught them many, many, MANY lessons about Himself through their disobedience. He'd proven His trustworthiness. Therefore, He asked them to step into the water and trust that He'd dry it up. He asked them to obey.

In so many ways, God has proven His faithfulness to me. He's cleared the path before asking me to cross so often. He's brought me out of the darkness that is recovery from betrayal. Now, it's time to move INTO something new.

I don't know what that is. I just know that writing is going to be a part of it.

Therefore, I'm beginning the process! I'm offering the Lord my sacrifice of obedience to Him. I don't know where that will lead. I'm beyond grateful, however, because He's taught me this much: *When He calls me TO, He always prepares me FOR.*

I pray that everything God has taught me will bless every reader of this book. I'm hopeful that my pain and discomfort will be used to encourage you in your walk with God. Adultery may not be something you are familiar with. However, I'll bet you have struggles of your own. If God has brought you OUT of difficulty, I just know it's because He wants to move you into something new. It may not be simple, but you can do it in the power of His Holy Spirit.

Let's do it together! Step into the water and *MOVE!* Trust that God will remove the obstacle when we step right into the middle of it. There are wonders waiting, and I believe obedience to the same commands God gave Joshua could be the key to experiencing the blessings God has prepared for us.

> *Then Joshua said to the people, "Consecrate yourselves, for tomorrow the Lord will do wonders among you"* (Joshua 3:5).

Day 1:
End It NOW!

Read Deuteronomy 34

I remember when I first started reading for pleasure. I was a married, adult woman. To the dismay of my sweet mother who has always loved a good book and many high school teachers that continued assigning novels I merely skimmed, I refused to enjoy reading prior to my early twenties. At that time, though, I discovered some very talented Christian fiction authors and I was hooked. One Saturday, I began that first book. After reading straight through two days and ENTIRELY too late on Sunday night, I finished the book. I couldn't put it down because I HAD to know how it ended. I quickly realized there was a huge problem with the way I read books. They were over too quickly and I was always sad to come to the end.

The first time I read through Deuteronomy completely, I was equally upset over the ending we read today. After spending so much time with Moses through Exodus and Deuteronomy, it's just hard to tell him, "goodbye." On top of that, his ending seems so unfair. He'd led ungrateful Israelites through the desert for forty years, and he didn't even get to enter God's Promised Land. But, as sad as I was for Moses, I was equally nervous for Joshua. Can you imagine inheriting the leadership role after someone like Moses?

> *Since then, no prophet has risen in Israel like Moses, whom the LORD knew face to face* (Deuteronomy 34:10).

In everyone—Joshua, the Israelites, ME (the reader)—lies the desire to hang on to Moses. He was a great leader and he'd done amazing things. However, we will see through the book of Joshua that God was ready to do NEW things for the Israelites. Sometimes, old things must die to make room for new things to be born. And, while that can be exciting, it can also be hard!

It's tough to say goodbye to friendships, communities, homes, churches, etc. Let's be honest. It can be downright impossible! I'll go a step further and acknowledge that ending relationships with less tangible things that have been even more a part of life (hopes and dreams) could be the most difficult goodbyes of all. If I had to determine the greatest struggles of my journey through life until this point, it would be the times I was forced to experience the disappointment of *dying* expectations. There are people MISSING from my life today, and I never dreamed something could have taken them from me. Their departures signify the *crushing* of hopes and expectations. Life is HARD, and *endings* are a huge part of the difficulty.

As painful as they were, some of those deaths created space for new hopes and dreams to be born. I believe the story of Moses and Joshua depicts this truth perfectly. God had GIANT plans for Joshua, but he and the Israelites had to end it with Moses first. According to this chapter in Deuteronomy, they may have been forced to move forward into God's plan without Moses AND without really knowing what happened to Moses. Deuteronomy says, "his eye was not dim nor was his vigor abated." Yet, he died and God buried him.

Therefore, Deuteronomy ends, Joshua begins, and I wonder if our main character was grieving the loss of a mentor and scared to death to lead God's people when Moses left such "big shoes to fill." Didn't the poor guy need some closure? Probably. But, he made the choice to move forward with God. It was time for Joshua to step INTO the plans God had for him even though the plans appeared scary, uncertain, and maybe even impossible.

You and I must also choose. God has plans for our lives but the fulfillment of those plans won't necessarily be easy. Some of God's plans for me have been ushered in through much pain. Some of the pain could have been avoided *and God used it anyway.* In kingdom economy, NOTHING is wasted when we allow Him to be in control. Where do you need to bid a farewell today? Give it to God, because He can be trusted with it. Then, be ready to move on with Him. I love the commentary in my Bible at the start of the book of Joshua,

> *"Joshua was victorious in destroying the Canaanites because of a new breed of Israelite; those who took God at His word. The main purpose of the Book of Joshua was to show how God kept His original promise to Abraham and how the wicked were expelled. The children of those who had been redeemed out of Egypt by the blood of the Passover were now claiming the blessing of that redemption"* (Hebrew-Greek Key Word Study Bible, NASB, 290).

The Israelites that crossed into the Promised Land were required to let go of Moses and follow Joshua. They were forced to believe God would carry them even though some of their expectations had been crushed. They were a "new breed of Israelite," so they claimed the blessing God had for them across the Jordan.

Today, ask God to show you where you are hanging on to people, circumstances, or expectations that He wants to remove in order to bring something new to your heart and life. Express to Him the fear and sadness you may have in saying goodbye. Don't hold back. Your loving Father knows your heart anyway, and He can handle it. Then, express your desire to claim your blessings. *I've traveled with God enough to know that if He's asking you to make a sacrifice, His plans on the other side are far greater than anything He's called you to give up.* He can be trusted with *every* relationship, *every* plan, *every* hope and expectation. Be a person that takes God at His word and watch Him carry you to places you've never believed you could go.

Across the pages of this study, let's join together to become a "new breed" of believer. Our God is on the MOVE and I want us to join Him. Today, start the journey with a prayer of commitment to step into this new season no matter what it costs. If He's asked you to close a door, bury a dream, or grieve an unmet expectation, lay it on the altar with JOY. Trust Him with the WHY and let's start moving towards full and abundant life in Him.

> *Now to Him who is able to do exceeding abundantly beyond all that we ask or think, according to the power that works within us, to Him be the glory in the church and in Christ Jesus to all generations forever and ever. Amen* (Ephesians 3:20).

Day 2:
Arise!

Read Joshua 1:1–5

Moses, My servant, is dead; now therefore arise, cross this Jordan, you and all this people, to the land which I am giving to them, to the sons of Israel (Joshua 1:2).

I believe God's Word is living and active. I also believe it is perfect. In other words, I trust that, inspired by God, the writers of each book of the Bible wrote exactly the words God intended to be scripted on His Holy pages. No words have been left out and no extras have been included. Since the Lord spoke to Joshua saying, "Arise," I'm assuming Joshua was NOT arisen.

During the first year of healing from adultery, there were days I literally did not feel like I could get out of my bed. I didn't necessarily want to lie around all day. However, I couldn't tell myself to do anything different. Praise God most days weren't like that. Anyone that has lived through trauma knows that there are days when you just don't feel like rising to the occasion.

Later in our recovery, I felt stronger. I'd seen God move in amazing ways and I knew He was going to see us through the process of complete redemption. However, I still had days where *rising* to the calling of that particular day was a lot to ask. I experienced fear of doing the wrong thing and sometimes felt paralyzed in the decision-making process. I needed the Lord to call me to arise in Him and do what He'd called me to do at that moment in His plan. I needed a clear and imperative word for the *one* day I was facing. That's all I could handle.

The Bible doesn't tell us how Joshua was *feeling* in chapter one of this book. The Lord's instruction to him is insightful, though. He gave Joshua a few instructions, but He began with, "Arise." The Israelites had wandered in desert darkness for forty years. In the book of Joshua, God was ready to move them into their promised land. First, their leader had to GET UP! The only preparation God asked of Joshua at that moment was to get on his feet.

Yes! Moses was dead and that's sad! If there is sadness, hurt, pain, fear, anxiety, or depression in your life, *name it.* God did. He didn't ignore Joshua's reality in the moment. He called it out.

Yes! The task ahead was huge, and Joshua probably felt unprepared. Perhaps he was having a panic attack of sorts. I'm certain there was anxiety over having to lead as Moses led. Again, the Lord gave him the freedom to voice that concern.

The list of uncertainties could go on and on. The fact of the matter is, the Lord didn't need Joshua to have all of the answers. He just needed him to start, get going, and *begin!* On God's sovereign calendar, it was time for His children to move into their promised land. First, He asked their new leader to prepare to see Him do amazing and miraculous things.

What causes you to doubt that God can and will exert His power over your life today? I don't believe we are supposed to shove all of life's negative experiences into the garbage and hope the memories just disappear. There's no way I could simply *forget* the negative circumstances of my life. God's way encourages me to call out to Him and name the sadness, fear, anxiety, or difficulty. I can give it to Him and cooperate with Him to redeem the mess in a way that fulfills His plans for my life. However, I can't remain in the darkness of the struggle. I can't use the negative memory or unfortunate event to stay down. I must ARISE!

You must too! There's a promised land waiting.

There are battles to be won.

There are missions to be accomplished.

We will never know the fullness of God's awesome power in and through our lives if we don't get up and get started.

> *Every place on which the sole of your foot treads, I have given it to you, just as I spoke to Moses* (Joshua 1:3).

God's plan was to bless His children through Joshua. His plan could not be thwarted, but Joshua could have missed his participation in it. If he hadn't answered the call to "arise," the sole of his foot wouldn't have treaded *any* piece of new land. The same goes for you and me.

> *Blessed be the God and Father of our Lord Jesus Christ, who has blessed us with every spiritual blessing in the heavenly places in Christ* (Ephesians 1:3).

So, today, call out to your God. Trust that He has plans for you even if you can't see them yet. First and foremost, God desires that we seek Him and behold His glory. Whatever life event has you 'lying down,' hear Him calling you to life in Him. Stand in the security of Christ, our solid ground, and hear Him say:

> *Just as I have been with Moses, I will be with you; I will not fail you or forsake you* (Joshua 1:5).

Day 3
Fear Not!

Read Deuteronomy 31:1–13

This morning, I'm forcing myself to write. My heart and mind are in a thousand different places. Scotty and I have been surprised by God's moving this week, and we have some choices to make. We don't have to make ANY decisions yet. We simply have to be *open* to following God if He continues to move us along this particular path. It would be a good path! It's just a different path. If I'm honest with myself, the unsettled feeling I have that's causing my lack of focus is simply FEAR.

Moses knew the Israelites would also struggle with fear as they journeyed. In our reading passage today, he prepared them for his departure, announced Joshua's leadership status, and encouraged them NOT to be afraid.

The boldness Moses had in encouraging Joshua and the Israelites is interesting to me. He had not crossed the Jordan for himself. He didn't know what they would face or WHO they would face. Undoubtedly, God's children would encounter obstacles Moses couldn't have expected. Yet, he very strongly insisted they go, *without* fear and trembling. How was Moses able to confidently assure God's people of victory when the details of that victory were just as unknown to him?

I believe we could read through Exodus and list numerous reasons Moses' last words to the Israelites were filled with pleadings to trust God in all things. In the exodus account, we'd find many, many times that God made and kept a promise to Moses. Moses felt comfortable assuring the Israelites to fearlessly trust God would do what He said He would do, because he'd lived a lifetime of seeing God do exactly what He said He'd do. Praise God! He keeps His word because He is faithful. He can't be anything else. In his words to Joshua, Moses highlighted the most important thing we need to remember about our God:

> *And, the LORD is the one who goes ahead of*
> *you; He will be with you. He will not fail you*
> *or forsake you. Do not fear or be dismayed*
> (Deuteronomy 31:8).

The Israelites could move forward without fear because God was going ahead of them and would move with them. He'd promised them victory and that could have been enough. God promised to accompany them along the way, though. Joshua and God's people weren't going into battle with only the promise of victory. Their Creator and Heavenly Father committed to join them every step of the way.

Today, I'm facing a number of uncertainties. If I spend even as little as five minutes thinking about the details of our questions, my energy is drained, and I am a mess. Then, guilt and frustration set in. I am forty-one years old. I have walked a journey with the Lord. He's made so many promises and kept every single one. Beyond that, He's never left me to fend for myself. So, why am I here again? Why am I allowing myself to fear unknowns? I cannot answer without making too many excuses. But, I am comforted that our hero, Joshua, must have had a similar weakness. I know this because of three verses in the first chapter of Joshua:

> *Be strong and courageous, for you shall give this people possession of the land which I swore to their fathers to give them. Only be strong and very courageous; be careful to do according to all the law which Moses My servant commanded you; do not turn from it to the right or to the left so that you may have success wherever you go . . . Have I not commanded you: Be strong and courageous! Do not tremble or be dismayed for the LORD your God is with you wherever you go* (Joshua 1: 6–7, 9).

It seems I'm in good company with my issue of fear. However, as we'll soon see, Joshua's fear did not stop him from moving forward with the Lord. And, I don't want my fear to stop me.

How about you? What causes fear to creep in and steal your joy, sway your focus, or side-track your calling? Through the power of the Holy Spirit, the Lord is with you, believer, *wherever* you go. Nothing can stand against our great God. So, what are we waiting for? It's time to believe God can do it (whatever "it" is for you) and act according to that belief!

Right now, I'm praying that God gives wisdom to acknowledge any fear that threatens to hold you back. I'm asking that every person reading these words is granted the courage necessary to move forward with the Lord. May God grant you a desire to seek Him and His will that is greater than any fear. You go with courage, because you will never go alone!

> *So do not fear, for I am with you; do not be dismayed, for I am your God. I will strengthen you and help you; I will uphold you with my righteous right hand* (Isaiah 41:10).

Day 4:
Assume Your Position

Read Joshua 1:10–18

Finally, on day four, we hear from Joshua himself. Until this point, we've had to assume what he was thinking and feeling. We've heard the Lord speak to Joshua, but Joshua has been completely quiet.

In today's reading, though, Joshua spoke to the officers of the people of Israel. He spoke with authority. He spoke with the tone of victory. Joshua commanded his officers to prepare for a victory.

Speaking things out loud, especially to powerful people, is unnerving. Goals and plans can remain hidden until they are spoken to another person or group of people. Once the vision is communicated, accountability becomes an issue. Other people will be checking in, determining progress, and evaluating follow through.

Several years ago, my husband and I decided we were going to homeschool our three children. God clearly led us to this decision in a way that didn't allow our refusal. We prayed about it for a while, and we knew it was the right choice. However, I didn't tell anyone about our decision for a long time. First, I knew our friends and some of our family would think we were crazy. I suspected this reaction, because I'd thought several of my own friends who'd chosen to homeschool were crazy. The main reason I didn't share with anyone, though, is that I was nervous about announcing I was going to do something I wasn't positive I could actually do.

I had all sorts of reservations about homeschooling our children, but they all boiled down to one simple thought, "What if I can't do it?" I did not want to tell people too early because I was concerned with what they would think or say, if or when the day came that I had to march my kids right back to the school and confess I couldn't do what I'd set out to do.

I'm so impressed with Joshua's stand in this first chapter. He didn't "hem-haw" around (as we say in the South) by pulling a few people to the side to see what they thought about his plan. On the contrary, he spoke in commands to the officers of the people. There weren't any committee meetings or votes! Joshua knew what the Lord had asked him to do and he relayed the message to his people:

> *Pass through the midst of the camp and command the people, saying, "Prepare provisions for yourselves, for within three days you are to cross this Jordan, to go in to possess the land which the LORD your God is giving you, to possess it"* (Joshua 1:11).

So, how do you think the Israelites even began to *prepare provisions* to cross the Jordan? They had no idea what they were walking into. Therefore, they had no idea how to prepare for it. The same was true for me once I let my world know that our kids would be leaving the school system to be taught by me at home. Man, were there stares, questions, and looks of, "you've lost your mind." The scariest part of all was that I was sure they could be right. My one and only comfort was the fact that God had clearly called, so I trusted He would clearly lead.

After Scotty's confession of adultery in 2011, our family was in distress. Our children didn't really know what all had happened, but that didn't matter. We were obviously fractured and in need of healing. In 2012, we moved to a new city. The fresh start was welcomed. However, the busyness of our schedules still didn't allow us the time we needed to heal and grow as a family. God's leading us to homeschool would give us space in the schedule to do what we needed to do. I understood that, but I still didn't know how to prepare for it. We were forced to move forward with God's plan without actually knowing how.

I believe the Israelites must have had similar feelings and emotions. Possibly, they moved forward in obedience *only* because they knew what it was like to live with the consequence of disobedience.

We will get to the other side of the Jordan in order to see the 'how' of God's plan in Joshua. Today, I'm in a position to share some of the details on the other side of our homeschooling journey. After three years together, our children will return to school next year. My eyes are teary as I write, because our time together has been so precious! Let me first say that *everything* I was afraid of happening *did* actually happen; there were days I didn't feel like teaching and had to anyway, there were times my schedule at home didn't allow me to do some of the things I wanted to do, there were lessons to be taught that I didn't know how to teach, and I could list many more examples. I chose to homeschool only because God let me know it was right for us. But, there were still obstacles to overcome.

The blessings of our obedience, though, are too numerous to count. The fact that my heart is sad to consider the kids leaving each day for school is a testimony of God's faithfulness. Yes, teaching them was *hard.* Maybe that is what makes it so special. Each and every day, I've found myself in situations that were too demanding for me to handle. Yet, day after day, God used the good and the bad to chip away at the yuck in me pointing me to a better way. We are closer as a family unit because we chose a different path and trusted God with the outcome. Somehow, God used Scotty and me to prepare our children, not only emotionally and spiritually but also academically. The boys have passed their placement testing back into public school with flying colors. God is *SO* good!

Where do you need to verbally announce the direction you want your life to move under the guidance and direction of the Holy Spirit? Maybe you don't need an audience as large or as powerful as Joshua's. There is something to be said for accountability, though. If God is leading you to make some life changes, especially if the changes will require you to live life differently than you've ever lived before, *let someone know!* Don't keep it to yourself. Put it out there so others can help with follow through. God is an "on the go" God. Where are you going with Him?

One last thing. Did you catch how much time the Israelites had to prepare for the move? THREE DAYS! God made a promise to Abraham many years before. Then, He assured fulfillment in Moses. Since that time, God's people had experienced a harsh Pharaoh, miraculous plagues, parting of the Red Sea, provision in the desert, forty years of wandering in the desert, and the death of Moses. God's timing seemed to be in slow motion. Then, *suddenly,* the Israelites were told to make preparations for crossing the Jordan River in only three days.

God's clock is something we can't figure out but we can trust. Today, pray for His plans and for your heart. I know you want to follow God completely. That is a process. In it, we have to know when to sit and wait, when to wander with purpose, and when to get up and go! The only way to do that well is to follow Jesus *daily.* Cry out to Him right now and express your great need to know Him more so that you can live this life well. Please know that I am joining you in that cry.

> *For it is God who is at work in you, both to will and to work for His good pleasure* (Philippians 2:13).

Day 5:
Let Shame Go!

Read Joshua 2 (Focus on verses 15 through 24)

Today, let's talk about Rahab. Her character is an interesting one and all of us should have a few questions when reading about Rahab's life. The Bible gives her a title nearly every time she is listed—Rahab, the harlot.

Can you even imagine THAT being the way you are remembered forever? In fact, in verse one, she's named as "the harlot" before we even hear her name.

> *So they went and came into the house of the harlot whose name was Rahab and lodged there* (Joshua 2:1).

Prior to having children, I taught third grade. I loved it so much. During that time, if someone had referred to me as "the third grade teacher whose name is Mrs. Rogers," I probably would have been thrilled. I worked in a superb district and was surrounded by excellent teachers. So, if I was named first as THE teacher, I'm fairly certain I would have loved being remembered that way. I'm thinking Rahab wasn't as thrilled with her title. I don't really know how society worked back then as compared to now. But, I can't imagine there was a great sense of pride over the title "harlot."

I have to believe there were times Rahab let that title get the best of her. We weren't created for the life of a harlot. Therefore, even as an unbeliever, I assume Rahab despised her work and dealt with loads of guilt and shame. The consequences of her lifestyle, no doubt, created chaos in her mind and soul. On this particular day, though, her shame did not get the best of her. These spies clearly represented freedom to her and she wasn't afraid to ask for help.

This is boldness at its boldest in my opinion. The Bible doesn't lead me to believe harlotry was a past occupation for Rahab. It appears that this was her occupation at the time the story took place. So, HOW did she abandon shame long enough to ask the spies for salvation? No sooner had the men sent by the king of Jericho left her presence that she rushed to the men of God and asked for protection. She pleaded with them. Eventually, they granted her request.

Let me take a moment to confess a little. I'm NOT a perfect person. I have to live in my skin and I know I have major flaws. I stumble in areas that seem to be recurring and that frustrates me. But, praise God's glorious name, I haven't lived in a pit of sexual and lifestyle sin. Truly, that's a praise to God. I know I don't have the power within myself to have kept myself OUT of that kind of bondage. However, I live with someone who has fallen to sexual sin and is working with God to restore and recover all that was lost. I've seen firsthand what sin (specifically sexual sin) can do to a life. The guilt is real. The shame is debilitating. It has a way of rearing its ugly head and making a person believe his sin is too great to ever attempt to live outside of that bondage.

33

Did Rahab suffer from that self condemnation? If she did, she found the strength to overcome it when it mattered. She rushed to the spies and asked for help. Maybe she didn't think she deserved it, but that didn't stop her from asking. She didn't let the pain, the guilt, or the shame keep her from making a request to be freed before Jericho was demolished.

We will never know what might have happened if Rahab, the harlot, allowed shame to keep her from God's blessing, but we do know what happened because of her boldness.

First, her life was spared. She asked to be spared. The spies granted her request and then some. All of her family that was in her house at the time Israel took their land would be spared from destruction.

The next blessing of Rahab's boldness can be read in the book of Matthew:

> *"and to Salmon was born Boaz by Rahab ..."*
> (Matthew 1:5).

That verse may seem like nothing to you, unless you realize this is the chapter that names Christ's lineage. Rahab, the harlot, is part of the line of Christ! Can you think of a higher calling? If Rahab was alive and a believer today, her own church might tell her she's disqualified from teaching Sunday school, serving, or leading in any way. Yet, God didn't disqualify her from being part of the lineage that ushered His Son into this world.

Finally:

> *By faith Rahab the harlot did not perish along with those who were disobedient, after she welcomed the spies in peace* (Hebrews 11:31).

Well, now it's just getting *crazy*! Rahab, *the harlot,* made it into the Hebrews Hall of Faith. Amazing! What exactly was her great act? **She believed God!**

Somehow, Rahab overcame her unbelieving past, her sin-filled present, and her fear for the future by *faith*. She simply believed God could save her. Though, she first had to believe she was worth saving.

Later in this Joshua chapter, Rahab "tied the scarlet cord in the window" (2:21), and I wonder if she felt a little bizarre doing it. I'm imagining she had conversations with herself about what she would say if anyone asked what she was doing. I feel like she'd know she couldn't tell them, because no one would believe that God would save any of the Canaanites much less Rahab, the harlot.

He did, however! Rahab's life tells the story of salvation and redemption. Your life could too. I don't know your past, but God does. Maybe you, like my husband, committed horrible sin *after* confessing and professing Jesus as Lord of your life. If no one has said it to you before, hear me say, "I'm sorry." If the Holy Spirit was living in you while you lived in sin, you were miserable in the mess. Allowing the lies of the Devil to speak louder than the truth of a merciful God is damaging. It's time to listen to the right voice. The scarlet cord is Christ. His death and resurrection made it possible for all of us to stand in His forgiveness and live a life of freedom.

It's hard to move forward with God while hanging on to past defeats. It's time to let God have them. Trade your shame for His salvation. From the Hebrews Hall of Faith, I believe Rahab (the harlot) would scream that trusting God for freedom is a bold act of faith! Receiving God's press over our own is tough when we know how many bad choices have been made. I believe Rahab, the faithful, would say it's worth it. Now, you believe it! Hold fast to the scarlet cord of Christ's love and LIVE.

And you were dead in your trespasses and sins, in which you formerly walked according to the course of this world, according to the prince of the power of the air, of the spirit that is now working in the sons of disobedience. But God, being rich in mercy because of His great love with which He loved us, even when we were dead in our sin, made us alive together with Christ (by grace you have been saved) ... (Ephesians 2:1–2, 5).

Day 6:
Tell Your Story!

Read Joshua 2:1–14

It's so hard for me to begin today's devotion without going back to Numbers 13. So badly, I want to spend some time reflecting on Moses' plan to send spies into the Promised Land. He sent twelve spies. Ten came back with a bad report. Two, Joshua and Caleb, returned with the report that they should go and take their land. Majority ruled, fear took over, and the Israelites wandered in the desert for forty years because they believed the negativity and doubted God's power. Fast forward to Joshua 2, in which Joshua determined only two spies were necessary. Surely, he had the previous ten on his mind.

Two spies caused quite a commotion, though. I don't know how much time elapsed, but it sure seems that no sooner had these spies arrived in Jericho, their presence was known. In a time where there was no Fox News, no Facebook, and no Google updates, two men (maybe boys) traveled into Jericho and word was sent to the king. Not only that, their visit apparently created a movement of fear because the king sent his people to Rahab to get the spies.

What in the world? How could the king of Jericho be so moved by two outsiders? Honestly, what could two men (even if they were big and strong men) do to a nation? I believe Rahab's words to the spies answer these questions well:

> *I know that the LORD has given you the land,*
> *and that the terror of you has fallen on us,*
> *and that all the inhabitants of the land have*
> *melted away before you. For we have heard*
> *how the LORD dried up the water of the Red*
> *Sea before you when you came out of Egypt,*
> *and what you did to the two kings of the*
> *Amorites who were beyond the Jordan, to*
> *Sihon and Og, whom you utterly destroyed.*
> *And when we heard it, our hearts melted and*
> *no courage remained in any man any longer*
> *because of you; for the LORD your God, He*
> *is God in heaven above and on earth below*
> (Joshua 2:9–11).

God's work in the lives of HIS people, the Israelites, was so miraculous that even non-believers heard of it. God's movement in the humble lives of people is transforming and Rahab's words demonstrated that fact. Her people had been moved to fear and their hearts melted over the idea that the people of the One, True God were headed in Jericho's direction.

How has God worked in your life? I'm not anticipating that anyone has a story similar to the Red Sea drying up before you, but I know He's done wonders in your life if you've walked with Him for any amount of time. I want to encourage you to spend some time today writing out memories of God's powerful displays of His presence in your life. Make your list, check it twice, and thank Him for those faith-building experiences.

These experiences are part of your testimony and God intends for you to share them. Quite simply, a testimony is our tool to share the Gospel of Redemption with the world. Yet, so many times, our life-changing experiences with God accompany failures. Often, we don't share how God redeemed our messes because we are viciously fighting to hide those embarrassing and hurtful life experiences from those we know.

I can assure you, there is NOTHING fun about sharing the hurt of adultery in my marriage. Not. A. Thing! But, for almost five years now, God has been moving and working through our mess in amazing ways. He has performed miracles in us, through us, and all around us! We simply handed him our ugly situation and asked as best we could for healing, restoration, and redemption. He chose to honor our request. The details have been uncertain at times. We haven't fully 'arrived.' However, He's proven faithful time and time again. We know He can be trusted!

In all of this, I have found that no matter how hard it is to tell my story, others must know it because it is a true and current desert story. It's my own story of deliverance to freedom, provision in poverty, and victory over the enemy. When I remember my story, my own fear of failure melts. When I share my story, other "Rahabs" might be empowered to ask for their own miracles while an unbelieving world trembles at the power of God.

Sadly, we do live in the Fox News, Facebook, and Google world. Rather than sharing our struggles and failures readily, we are tempted to hide and pretend. Instead of embracing our humanity and fragility, we'd rather fight to appear strong. Meanwhile, the world is *dying* to know how to overcome weakness and failure when it seems others have it all together.

I'm not a scholar of the book of Revelation, but, there is a verse that was recently shared with me and I feel convicted to take it to heart:

> *And they overcame him (the accuser of the brethren) because of the blood of the Lamb and because of the word of their testimony, and they did not love their lives even to death* (Revelation 12:11).

The word of our testimony is a weapon to be used against the accuser. Could it be the thing you are fighting to hide and cover might be the message that will help you overcome the accuser? Could your message empower others to tremble at the power of our mighty God?

I don't want to spoil the ending of the story for anyone who may be reading Joshua for the first time, but the Israelites do destroy their enemy. They do take over the land of Jericho in bold pursuit of God's plan for their lives. In today's passage, we've read the first step in their enemy's defeat. They trembled at what God had already accomplished in the lives of the Israelites and they feared what might happen next.

Your enemy is no different. Satan knows what God has done in your past. He even knows that God will be victorious in your future. Although the cross of Christ was Satan's ultimate defeat, he has a number of victories threaded all throughout our testimonies. I bet he's so proud of those victories *until* we, as believers, acknowledge our God's miraculous work even in the humiliation of defeat. You better believe his heart 'melts' when we determine our testimonies won't make us hide in guilt and shame. When we look back over our temporary failures and decide they will actually be a tool to share God's glory with others, I believe Satan trembles and is reminded he's one step closer to his ultimate and eternal failure.

Today, own *your* story. I'm sure it's full of good *and* bad. No doubt, there's pretty *and* ugly. God will redeem it all. Nothing is wasted! In His sovereign way, He will make a beautiful design with *all* of the pieces. And maybe, just maybe, He will allow your testimony to empower other believers to overcome.

> *For I am not ashamed of the gospel, for it is the power of God for salvation to everyone who believes, to the Jew first and also to the Greek* (Romans 1:16).

Day 7:
Consecrate Yourself!

Read Joshua 3:1–5

I am on a real journey with the Lord. Truly, it's an adventure. I've believed in God since the age of seven. For most of my life, I have lived with a sincere awareness of His presence. However, God has recently drawn me into deeper waters with Him. He's asked me to trust Him more heavily than I've ever needed to before. I have, because it's the *only* thing I could do in all honesty.

I've followed God into waters that are over my head, because that is where He has been. In the darkest moments of life, I knew I couldn't even manage the kiddie pool if God wasn't there with me. I've discovered something in this scary place. *True living* is done in the depths and darkness of life. Having to depend on God for every little breath seems to be the life I was meant to live. For as long as I am breathing, I want to lead others into the deep to find abundant life with God in Christ.

In our Bible reading today, I can literally feel the Israelite nervousness. I can hear the shaky voices as they discuss their next steps. But, I also sense some excitement. There had to be a thrill in the realization that something new was just ahead. The time of wandering in the wilderness was ending and new beginnings were on the horizon.

Soon after Scotty confessed his sin to me, we realized that God might call us to relocate. I had mixed emotions. Sure, at the earliest moments, I wanted Him to move us to something new. There was fear in that thought and even a little anger in the idea of a move. The town we lived in had been home to us for nineteen years. We had friendships and memories I was afraid to give up. I was bitter that I might have to. Emotionally, I was in a crisis and didn't really know what I wanted. In my mind, I secretly weighed out which would be more difficult. I found great comfort in the fact that God already knew His plans for us. We just needed to wait and see. We waited for what seemed like forever. Suddenly, He laid out His plan before us. We had to go, and we went quickly.

As I think about all of the emotions the Israelites must have experienced, I'm sure the one that fought for first place at all times was, "how do we do this?" Thankfully, their instructions included only one main directive— FOLLOW THE ARK.

The presence of the Lord would go before them, and the Israelites needed to follow after it. The reason they had to follow is because they were going a way they'd never been before. I don't care how brave of a person you are, that is a scary thought. It's human nature. We like *well-known* ways. Naturally, we always seek the familiar road.

The Hebrew word for "ways" has depth to it. More than just a path, it signifies a *pattern* for life. The use of this word suggests that God's chosen people weren't just asked to physically travel a new path. Their *patterns* for living needed to be adjusted. Now, that's a tough realization. To know that 'the way we've always done it' may not work anymore is hard to accept at times.

> *Then Joshua said to the people, "Consecrate yourselves, for tomorrow the LORD will do wonders among you"* (Joshua 1:5).

The Hebrew word for "consecrate" is qadash. It's a word that means, "set apart, dedicated, to treat as holy, or to show oneself as holy." I've read a number of books and passages that discuss "consecrating oneself." There are many ideas about its meaning. Fasting from food, giving up television, or changing a friend group are opportunities to consecrate yourself before the Lord. All of these require us to *give something up* as a way to acknowledge God and His holiness in our lives. Sacrifice for sanctification is a good start.

What if there's more to it? I've done all of these things in an attempt to ready myself for a new work from the Lord. He's always faithful to honor my attempts to follow Him more closely. I just feel the circumstances of this passage are too huge to imagine the act of giving something up could prepare the Israelites for the *new* that God was preparing.

As we packed up and prepared to leave our little home and community after nineteen years of comfort, **my consecration had to be an acknowledgement that His way was better than my way no matter what that meant.** This confession had to be my consecration, because I didn't know what we'd find. There were too many uncertainties.

Did I ever consider fasting to search for God's way? YES!

Were there times when I felt called to give up something (food, television, activity) to focus on God's will for me? Absolutely!

However, yielding to God's authority over every situation, trusting that His way is best even when it looks different than I'd like, and resting in the fact that He knows the outcome before I ever begin the journey is also consecrating.

Experiencing God's best for us will always require admitting that He rules. When the way is different and the path is unknown, that confession becomes especially necessary. Otherwise, we will miss the gift, the provision, or our new direction.

What if *tomorrow* (meaning your future) the Lord wants to do wonders among you? I believe we serve a God and Father that desires to bless His children. Sometimes, we have to wade through obstacles first. Often, we must fight through battles to experience His victory. Consecrate yourself *unto* Him today by confessing your great need *for* Him. Acknowledge that you don't know the way and ask Him to show you where patterns of thinking are hindering your experience of His goodness in your life. Then, get ready! I don't know what newness He wants to bring your way. , but I am positive you don't want to miss it.

> *Behold, I will do something new, now it will spring forth; Will you not be aware of it? I will even make a roadway in the wilderness and rivers in the desert* (Isaiah 43:19).

Day 8:
Begin!

Read Joshua 3:6–7 and Deuteronomy 28:1–14

As I stare at a blank screen and a lone cursor, I'm struck by this thought, *beginnings aren't easy!*

I know last week we talked about the difficulty with endings. In so many ways they are tougher than I can describe, but getting started is a challenge on so many levels. Starting over and participating in a 'reset' is a scary thing.

In Joshua, that is exactly what God was announcing. He told Joshua that He was going to *begin* to exalt him in the eyes of the Israelites. He did not proclaim, "I will exalt you in the eyes of Israel." Obviously, it was going to be a process and processes must *begin* somewhere.

Every great story has a beginning.

A delicious recipe begins with one ingredient.

Deep, long-lasting relationships start with an introduction.

A change in lifestyle begins with one deliberate step in a *different* direction.

If Joshua's message was my message from God, I hope I'd receive this word with a sense of confidence and assurance. However, I'm afraid (history being my number one indicator) I would have been overtaken by a spirit of, "How, Lord? Tell me *NOW!*"

For me, that's the struggle with processes. I want to be instructed on the 'how' from the start. I want to promise the Lord I will follow through *when* He shows the exact steps I'll be following. Many times, God just says, "Amy, let's begin," and I'm forced to simply get going. One step after another... *just begin.*

I remember leaving the counseling office after Scotty and I met to discuss his unfaithfulness. I left with a dear friend and Scotty went to be alone. I knew when we parted that I wasn't leaving our marriage. Even though I was angry and hurt, God allowed me to see Scotty's heart. I knew he was repentant and we'd stick it out. During the couple of hours we were apart, I shared raw and real emotions with my friend. I talked to family on the phone. I cried a lot and wished I was not being faced with the huge task of rebuilding a marriage and family. At the end of a few hours, though, I knew it was time to get back to my husband and get started. On what, I did not know!

My friend drove me across town to Scotty. He was sitting, reflectively, beside a small, neighborhood lake. I knew he'd been praying, crying, and probably battling all sorts of destructive thoughts. As I walked towards him, I felt a sense of, "here we go," in my spirit. At thirty-six years old, I'd barely figured out how to be married. I had absolutely no history from which to draw knowledge on 'fixing' a marriage. But, I knew we had to begin.

That's why I love our Deuteronomy 28 passage:

> *Now it shall be, if you will diligently obey*
> *the LORD your God, being careful to do all*
> *His commandments which I command you*

today, the LORD your God will set you high above all the nations of the earth. And all these blessings shall come upon you and overtake you if you will obey the LORD your God. (Deuteronomy 28:1–2).

My faithful God assured my spirit during those early moments that our marriage would not only be restored but would be made stronger than ever before. I had the confidence of Joseph in Genesis 50:20, "you meant evil against me, but God meant it for good in order to bring about this present result, to preserve many people alive." What I didn't know was HOW He would do it.

Today, I'm glad I didn't know what the process would be on that first day of rebuilding. In the beginning, I didn't need to know all of the steps He would take us—on some days, CARRY US—through. I couldn't have handled it all. On that day, I only needed to hear, "be careful to do all His commandments which I command you *today.*"

In other words, *just begin.* It takes courage to start on a new path. It takes faith to see it through. The outcome is blessing, though. God's Word in Deuteronomy assures He will bless our daily obedience. I don't know how He will do it in your life. I am positive there will be highs with lows, fair weather with storms, and straight paths with obstacles. But, I am sure that His outcomes are always the ones we want. His gifts, even when they look different than we'd like, always bring about the changes we need.

On the third day of our reading, God announced the plan to *begin* to exalt Joshua among the Israelites. What could He be ready to begin in your life, in my life, on THIS day? Even this far into our recovery, I know God is beginning new things each day. I don't always know what they are. Thankfully, I always know what MY part in them will be.

I must yield to His authority, His goodness, and His sovereignty acknowledging that His way is the best way.

I must carefully obey all of His commands to me this day.

Today, I must begin the journey *forward* with Him.

> *The Lord is the portion of my inheritance and my cup; Thou dost support my lot. The boundary lines have fallen to me in pleasant places; Indeed, my heritage is beautiful to me. I will bless the Lord who has counseled me; Indeed, my mind instructs me in the night. I have set the Lord continually before me; because He is at my right hand, I will not be shaken* (Psalm 16:5–8).

Day 9:
Recognize His Power!

Read Joshua 3:6–16

D on't you love that Joshua reads like a story? It IS a story, a true story, but often we miss that because our lessons hop all over the Bible. Reading a book of the Bible from start to finish allows our naturally skeptical hearts to see that God's Gospel of redemption has always played out in lives like yours and mine. Taking in the full script verse by verse gives us the opportunity to SEE the drama like a movie. So, let's picture this scene:

> *And it shall come about when the soles of the feet of the priests who carry the ark of the LORD—the LORD of all the Earth—shall rest in the waters of the Jordan, the waters of the Jordan shall be cut off, and the waters which are flowing down from above shall stand in one heap* (Joshua 3:13).

I can hear pleading in Joshua's speech. He was urging the Israelites to acknowledge God's power over all things. He wanted them to understand that THE God who created the Jordan River had authority over the water in it. The Lord of all the Earth was preparing to demonstrate His power over creation by causing water to STAND UP in one heap.

That's power! I'm imagining what it looked like, but I'm sure my picture doesn't compare to the real thing. The power of God's presence, contained in the ark of the covenant, was so strong that as soon as the priests carrying it stepped into the river, the water would literally back up and away.

Do you know that God's strong presence in the form of His Holy Spirit abides in YOU as a believer? The same authoritative power that caused river water (at full flood stage, by the way) to stand up in a heap, with the flow completely cut off, lives inside of Christ's followers.

I'd like to gently ask if you are currently living a life that exhibits that power. I'd also like to suggest that our world could be transformed if believers actively *trusted and believed* God's power is at work each and every day just as mightily as it was in Joshua's time.

The Jordan River was an obstacle to God's people getting into Canaan, but God wasn't going to allow it to be a hindrance. Amazing things happened because God determined it was time to exert His power over the Israelite situation. Do you have a situation that could use God's power? Have your obstacles turned into hindrances?

I'm sad to say I've lived in defeat for a long time by hiding behind obstacles. I believed God for my salvation a long time ago. In August 2011, I whole-heartedly believed in His power to heal my marriage. For four years, we've experienced such victory in our family. The miracle has been just as awe inspiring as the parting of the Jordan River! God's power is FOR REAL, and I would tell my marriage story with that message any day. Even in those victories, though, defeat has been a way of life in other areas.

This is hard for me to share, but Scotty and I experience financial defeats on a daily basis. We've had struggles with money as long as we've been married, and most of them originated with poor decision making. The consequences of 2011 multiplied our anxiety and caused more financial deficits; we followed that fear into more terrible choices. In my mind, our finances represent an obstacle as big as the Jordan at flood stage. It's huge. I don't even like to look at it. I don't want to talk about it. I certainly don't care to step into it. So, for some time, we've witnessed the miracle of marriage victory while living the humiliating defeat of financial failure all at the same time. Why don't I pray boldly and expect God to provide victories in my financial issues too?

The book of Hebrews assures me that God is the same yesterday, today, and forever. So, the issue must be me. In my mind, I've reasoned that marriage is important to God, so He will show up powerfully to heal the mistakes in our family. I would never say it out loud, but my words and emotions demonstrate a belief that financial freedom is less important than marriage health to God. So, Scotty and I just continue working to right our financial wrongs on our own. Left to ourselves we ALWAYS mess things up! When will my stubborn heart learn?

The truth is, I have NO idea where, when, or how God determines it's time to act on behalf of His children. I can't find anywhere in scripture where I've ever been asked to know that information. It seems to me my job is to *believe* that He is God. He can do whatever He wants, however He chooses, and whenever He determines it's time.

Paul says it like this,

> *I pray that the eyes of your heart may enlightened so that you may know what is*

the hope of His calling, what are the riches of the glory of His inheritance in the saints, and **what is the surpassing greatness of His power toward us who believe, these are in accordance with the working of the strength of His might which He brought about in Christ, when He raised Him from the dead, and seated Him at His right hand in the heavenly place** ... (Ephesians 1:18–20).

Our finances are a mess! (I think I keep saying it because it feels good to confess.) It makes me crazy to think about it. Most days, I *feel* like the chaos is too far gone to fix. But, I don't think our financial restoration would require more strength and power than *raising Christ from the dead!* Because I'm not actively believing that, though, I'm experiencing daily defeat. Trusting God with active belief changes things. I'm currently studying Beth Moore's book, *Believing God.* This focus has convicted me to believe God in all things. She very clearly states what I'm trying to say:

Nothing on earth compares to the strength God willingly interjects into lives caught in the act of believing. . . . You have no need that exceeds His power.

In what battle are you experiencing defeat? You're reading this book daily, so I'm trusting that you've believed God for the salvation of your soul. But, have you taken Him at His word and given Him the opportunity to rule your life as Lord? Have you surrendered every single obstacle to freedom to Him? He is God and we are not! We're killing ourselves by attempting to right all wrongs and fix all messes. He's better at it. When the presence of the Lord stepped into the waters of the Jordan they stood up in a heap. Wouldn't you like to experience that power for yourself? I would!

Keep in mind, the Israelites had been in the desert for forty years. In this passage, they move and God acts, but we can't forget the history or the timeline. Our God isn't a genie in a bottle granting each of our wishes as we ask. Honestly, we wouldn't want that!

No. Our God is all knowing and sovereign. He *delights* in exerting His power into the lives of believers AS IS BENEFICIAL to His lifetime plans for that believer. Thankfully, we don't have to know all of those plans. We just trust Him with all things, step out in freedom and power, and our lives begin to exhibit a transformation that the world around us will notice.

> *... seeing that His divine power has granted to us everything pertaining to life and god-liness, through the true knowledge of Him who called us by His own glory and excel-lence* (2 Peter 1:3).

Day 10:
Stand Firm!

And the priests who carried the ark of the covenant of the LORD stood firm on dry ground in the middle of the Jordan while all Israel crossed on dry ground until all the nation had finished crossing the Jorda. (Joshua 3:17).

'm fairly certain the only appropriate response after reading this verse is, "FINALLY!" For forty years, God's people wandered in desert land. Prior to that, their ancestors had spent 400 years in slavery in Egypt. Quite simply, it was *TIME* for crossing into freedom.

Joshua's account states that the priests carrying the Ark of the Covenant were required to 'stand firm' in the middle of the Jordan *until* all of the Israelites had crossed. That seems simple enough. My reading says there were 6,000 or more crossing that day. That's only the men. I wonder how the priests felt as the multitude was crossing. Did it seem like they'd never see the end of the line? Could they have been worried it might take too long, allowing the water to fall and crush them in that spot? Did their legs grow tired and their shoulders feel 'the burn' as they stood firmly planted, following Joshua's command?

I can't answer those questions for the priests, but I can answer for myself. I have found it is often difficult to *stand firm* in the 'until' moments of life. Since most of life is a process, rarely do we set out to accomplish something and achieve the desired result immediately. Praise God, sometimes we get to see instant victories. More often, we are required to make a decision and then *stand* with resolve until completion.

In Hebrew, the phrase "stand firm" means to cause to stand in an upright position, to be fixed, or steadfast. For the priests in the Jordan River, this phrase and its definition obviously refer to a *physical* position. Literally, they were asked to *stand* in the middle of the Jordan, feet firmly planted, until all of Israel crossed over. More often, I believe life's processes require the grit and determination to *emotionally* remain upright and steadfast even when circumstances make it easier to lie down in defeat.

Currently, my husband and I are preparing to "cross over" into an area of promise fulfillment. Nearly five years ago, we began a journey of healing and restoration. God's promise, through His Word, was that He would work all things together for His good (Romans 8:28). We trusted that He would do it based on His Word and His history of faithfulness. Some days, trusting was that simple. Most days, well, it was not.

As we've attempted to stand firm in the Lord throughout our marriage recovery, career transitions, and financial struggles, there have been days (many, MANY days) that all I could manage was to remain in an upright position. Literally, I got *up* out of my bed and carried out the tasks that HAD to be done. *That was it!* During those days, my brain could not focus on how, when, or if we'd EVER move beyond the repetitive struggle. During those days, I'd grip tightly to my Hope and trust that He would move us toward His promises. As I look back, I see the dark days. I'm reminded of the times I didn't know if I could carry on. I was tired and worn and ready to give up. **But, God held on**. He caused us to stand upright and gave us the courage to remain steadfast. He filled us with belief that we "would see the goodness of God in the land of the living" (Psalm 28:13). Even in darkness, God gave us the ability to do more than just live. He allowed us to live with hope and determination. Now, we get to 'cross over' into a renewed and redeemed calling with Him, because wilderness wandering is over and new ministry is calling.

Are you simply 'hanging on'? In Joshua, there had to be a steadfast position, a firm standing, before there was a crossover. I believe it will be the same for us. Whatever the situation is, we must be willing to cry out to God for perseverance. Don't quit! Don't give up! And, for goodness sakes, DON'T simply survive the thing *forever*. In Christ, we get to thrive even in less than desirable circumstances. Oswald Chambers said:

> Tenacity is more than hanging on, which may be but the weakness of being too afraid to fall off. Tenacity is the supreme effort of a man refusing to believe that his hero is going to be conquered. . . . Remain spiritually tenacious (*My Utmost for His Highest*).

The hero of our marriage restoration and ministry redemption is God through Jesus Christ. I'm convinced that He is the Hero of all redemptive stories. I'd like to encourage you to confess your weakness to Him today. Express belief that He can take your weakness, apply His power, and dramatically change your situation. Yield to the Hero of your story. Tenacious hope in Him can't be defeated. Hold fast, dear friend. Stand firm and be ready to cross over!

For whatever was written in earlier times was written for our instruction that through perseverance and the encouragement of the Scriptures we might have hope (Romans 15:4).

Day 11:
Deal With It, Again!

Read Joshua 4:1–8

I hope you found the 'again' in your reading today. Joshua chose twelve men and told them to cross into the Jordan River *again* and take a memorial stone from the middle of the river. The command seems simple enough until I recognize that the *middle* of the Jordan was likely an uncertain spot. Undoubtedly, every single Israelite crossed the Jordan with held breath, clinched fists or teeth, and quick feet. I can't imagine anyone desired to hang out in the middle of the Jordan even if it was bone dry. I feel confident this spot in the journey was a scary place for them. Yet, Joshua chose men and asked them to 'cross again' for a stone to create a place for remembering the difficulty of the journey when they arrived in their land of promise.

Oh, how God's ways amaze me! Why couldn't those men pick up stones from the water's edge on their way *out of* the river? That's the point of victory, right? The *end* of the difficulty should be what we choose to mark in our mind's memory. Wouldn't God ask them to remember stepping onto dry ground *in* the land of their promise instead of the most terrifying point in the crossing, the uncertain middle?

Do you know why I think this way? It's likely my mind would choose to memorialize the crossing, the victory, and the END for the same reason yours would. I don't like pain and discomfort! Many times, I will dodge it at all cost. When I can't escape it, I usually attempt to *get over it* as quickly as possible and hope to never think about it again.

Truly, we all want a life free of pain and discomfort. It will never happen and we should be very thankful. Pain is important. Without it, we could do serious damage to ourselves and others. Pain teaches us lessons, trains us for future events, and humbles us in a way that problem-free living never could. Pain can be our ally when we let God teach us *through* it and mark our lives *by* it.

When my oldest son was a toddler, he had a serious curiosity with my curling iron. Any time it was plugged in, he was right there, trying to get in close and figure it out. I said, "HOT," over and over. Still, one day, I turned my head and he grabbed the heated barrel. His hand was only there a second, but it left a mark and he screamed for quite a while. As bad as that ordeal was, it would have been much worse if pain hadn't told Caleb to remove his hand from the curling iron. The pain actually saved his hand.

Pain also taught him never to do it again! When allowed to do its job, pain can be a pretty amazing instructor. So quickly, we try and forget the pain in our lives when God could use it to teach us valuable lessons. Our hurt, self-inflicted or caused by others and examined through God's wisdom, could be the perfect textbook to prepare us for the remainder of our journey towards abundant life in Him.

I won't pretend to know why God told Joshua to send those twelve men *again* to the middle of the Jordan to pick up memorial stones. In my own life, He's sent me *back* to uncomfortable emotions and memories of difficult situations so that I could *feel* the pain until it's taught what it was meant to teach. In those times, God has granted spiritual maturity that equips me for journeying on with more grace, mercy, and dependence on Him. ***Pain isn't easy.*** But, we are wise to give it the pause and the place it deserves in our lives if we want to experience more victory.

Could you be **brave** enough to wade through the hurt *again* with God showing you, teaching you, and building your faith through the difficult memory? I know it's counter intuitive. I realize it seems bizarre. But, what if there is a lesson there you've missed? What if future victories are dependent on the memorial stone you need to pick up from that particular hurt?

Do you know that I never had to tell Caleb not to grab my curling iron again? Isn't that amazing! I spent so many minutes, hours, and days begging him to stay away from that pain. He touched it once, and that was it! God is our loving parent. Sometimes, He steps back and allows us to make the wrong decision. I believe His desire in allowing the painful, earthly experience is to mark our great dependence on Him. If He's allowed and ordained some pain in your life, there's something to be learned. He is entirely too loving and wise to allow us to move on without completing the sanctifying work with Him.

If He's called you to 'cross again,' I want you to do it with courage and boldness. Walk right back to the difficult spot *with God* and grab your memorial stone. You can wait to set it up until you've landed in victory territory. Don't miss out on the beauty that can happen right in the middle of the discomfort. In Christ, we get to deal with all of our hurts knowing that He will use every bit of it for our good.

I don't know where God is moving you, but I know His purpose is that you *bear much fruit* in your home, job, and relationships. Fruit bearing is a difficult process that involves pruning. There's no easy, pain-free way to get from seed to flower, but there *is* beauty and abundance. Together, let's commit to cross *again* if God has some training for us. Remember, if He calls you to it, He'll take care of you in it.

> *Furthermore, we had earthly fathers to discipline us, and we respected them; shall we not much rather be subject to the Father of spirits and live? For they disciplined us for a short time as seemed best to them, but He disciplines us for our good that we may share His holiness. All discipline for the moment seems not to be joyful, but sorrowful; yet to those who have been trained by it, afterwards it yields the peaceful fruit of righteousness.* (Hebrews 12:9–11)

Day 12:
Pause When Necessary!

Read Joshua 4:9–24

After reading our scripture today, I don't know if I should cheer, weep, or crank up some praise and worship music. Please tell me you feel the same way! God's rebellious and wandering Israelites stepped out of the Jordan and the waters returned to their place. They set up camp first at Gilgal; I hope you're as fascinated as I am by the meaning of this word.

Every commentary and study I've read states that Gilgal (or *the* gilgal, which could likely be the more appropriate translation) means "circle." Scripture has already told of a time when God's people stood at a miracle at the water's edge. In Exodus, they escaped bondage by crossing the Red Sea parted by God. Shortly after, they again traded freedom for bondage. Forty years later, Joshua's account detailed their *full circle crossing.* Once again, the Israelites were rescued by God's hand of protection and given another chance to receive freedom.

I must say, there is an element of JOY and REWARD in full circles and second chances. For sure, we celebrate these experiences and gratefully vow not to waste them.

At this point in my life, though, I also recognize there is huge responsibility that accompanies a second chance.

Today, I pulled out my computer to write for the first time in two months. TWO MONTHS! It's been a LONG time. During this writing break, my family has actually begun our *full circle* experience. We've moved to Florida and my husband is in ministry again. We know beyond the shadow of a doubt that we are here *only* by the grace of God. We are completely humbled and extremely grateful He deemed us worthy of another chance. On THE DAY that Scotty began as family pastor, I planned to write this part of our Joshua adventure. I was so very excited because we have been living our own 'Gilgal' and I'd been looking forward to comparing it to the Israelites'. Every time I tried, though, I couldn't write a single word.

I can be extremely hard on myself, so I've felt pretty down about this lag in writing. Typically, I don't start things and leave them unfinished yet that's what I've done with this book for two months. I've been burdened by the fact that this is MY second chance, and I've wanted so badly to share it well. Therefore, I made it all about ME and how I share. Writing paralysis has been the result. Instead of pausing with the Lord and asking for more guidance, I've allowed my inability to put our journey into words STOP me from letting Him guide the process. I believe God issued a time to rest, relax, and pause after several of the hardest years of my life as the next step in His process. It seems enjoying my family, taking day trips to the beach, and lounging on occasion were planned obstacles before moving on. Today, God is speaking His grace to me. He's showing me that *a pause* is often *the most necessary* step in the process.

I don't know where you've been or where you are now in this journey. I do know that *God is always moving and working in our lives.* In His mercy, some of our new seasons are actually 'do overs.' If you're like me, the JOY of getting a second chance can be overshadowed by the *FEAR* of messing up again.

So, pause.

Reflect and relax.

Realize that yielding to His leading as your first responsibility is the only thing that protects freedom.

If needed, set up camp at your Gilgal and spend some time remembering the goodness of God to call you into fellowship with Him. Thank Him that He is the author of second chances. Ask Him to give you the humility to trust Him fully as you move through the life He's given.

Our reading this morning ended with Joshua's instruction to the Israelites to set up their memorial stones and prepare to tell future generations what they stand for. God's provision had *again* been supplied and others would need to hear about it. The same is true for us. If formulating that story requires a pause, we are wise to receive it. My own intermission has given time for God to prepare me, through the power of His Holy Spirit, to respond humbly and obediently. Only He can make the most of a full-circle experience.

> *Be still, and know that I am God; I will be exalted among the nations, I will be exalted in the earth* (Psalm 46:10).

> *Behold, I will do something new, Now it will spring forth; Will you not be aware of it? I will even make a roadway in the wilderness, Rivers in the desert* (Isaiah 43:19).

Day 13:
Respond Differently!

Read Joshua 5:1–3

I enjoyed a summer movie with my children this week. One of the last lines was quite catchy, "Every great story has three main parts: a beginning, an end, and the TWIST." Well, this is a twist if I've ever known one.

The Israelites safely crossed the Jordan River and Joshua gave instructions to tell future generations of the mighty work God did in saving their entire nation. Today's reading began with the announcement that surrounding nations have heard of God's work on behalf of His people. Just as is written in Rahab's account, *their hearts melted and there was no spirit in them any longer.*

I'm no war strategist! However, it seems to me this would be the perfect time to attack and attack BIG! Right? Surely, the appropriate response for God's people while those inhabiting the land God had promised to them are mighty afraid is to TAKE! THAT! LAND!

Here's the twist. God had a different strategy ... *circumcision!* God told Joshua to sharpen his knife and circumcise his soldiers. Even if you've read this portion of scripture a million times, please stop and think it through for a moment. As leader of these soldiers, shouldn't Joshua get some answers from God concerning this directive before taking it to the people? If all of the surrounding armies were able to get word explaining God's miraculous work for the Israelites, wouldn't they hear of their weakened state? If God's plan included circumcision for the men of Israel, why didn't God ask Joshua to do it *before* crossing into enemy territory?

Scripture perfectly records Joshua's response, *So, Joshua made himself flint knives and circumcised the sons of Israel* (vs.3). He didn't grumble or complain. He didn't ask a single question. On top of that, there is no record of a complainer in the group receiving the news. God said it. They did it. However, quick and quiet obedience wasn't always their response.

In Exodus, the Israelites responded very differently when Moses gave instruction from God. When the direction was uncomfortable or inconvenient to them, they grumbled heavily! Exodus is *full* of their complaints. They grumbled about everything and even longed for their place back in Egypt where they were slaves. Apparently, forty years in the desert experiencing the consequence of complaining and disobedience had destroyed the need to question God. They'd learned a lesson and had determined to trust God and His leader *even if* the directive seemed absurd.

Scotty and I understand this particular mindset. We spent quite a few years arguing our case to the Lord. We'd grumble and complain when things weren't going our way. We certainly wouldn't step out of our comfort zones unless everything lined up and made sense according to our standards. We had a plan, a timeline, and an ideal we were set on achieving. When life fell apart and the consequence of sin was heavy on our lives, we learned quickly that OBEDIENCE is always the appropriate response to

God! In the past couple of years, we've felt God calling us to do things that seemed so silly. We worried (temporarily) that our friends and family would judge us for our unreasonable choices. Then we remembered the results of operating in our own wisdom and determined that we would choose obedience no matter what!

When is the last time you felt God gave you a directive that didn't make sense in your situation? How often do you find yourself pointing out why YOUR plan would work better than His plan? Have you ever chosen to follow through with your plan rather than God's and learned of His wisdom the hard way?

I am currently in the phase of parenting that includes more complaining and questioning from our children than we've ever had before. With one child in the teenage years and the next approaching quickly, they have their ideas about how the days should go. If my plan interferes with their plan, we often have debates, questions, and usually a little complaining. They gather information and plead their case, because they don't trust that we, as parents, see a bigger picture. They can't submit when they don't believe our intentions are always for their good.

God is our perfect parent. He loves us more than any person ever will! His plans for us are good and His way is perfect. He never has to apologize for His direction in our lives. He sees the beginning, the end, and every twist in between. If He's asked you to do something that seems absurd and makes no sense at all in your situation, I believe the best response is Joshua's response:

> *So, Joshua made himself a flint knife* (obeyed the Lord's directive) *and circumcised the Israelites* (Joshua 5:3).

The first step in making the most of the second chance is to obey God fully in all things. Recently, I read that God's love language is obedience. If we say we love him, we WILL obey His commands completely and without complaint. When I'm in a dry season and feel like I'm not receiving guidance from the Lord, I can usually remember something He's asked me to do that I haven't obeyed or *fully* obeyed. God simply *will not* send us to the next step until we've humbled ourselves in obedience in the first step. **THIS is for OUR GOOD.**

Today, I want to believe God as my perfect parent! Disobedience will only lead to bondage and death. Obedience, even in the little things, leads to LIFE. *He sees you, friend!* He knows who you are, where you are, and where you will go. His directions today are perfectly aligned with the plans He has for tomorrow. At every twist and turn, I want my life story to read, "So, Amy obeyed the Lord," and I'm praying the same for you.

> *Does the LORD delight in burnt offerings and sacrifices as much as in obeying the LORD? To obey is better than sacrifice, and to heed is better than the fat of rams* (1 Samuel 15:22).

Day 14:
Allow the Wounding to Make You Different!

Read Joshua 5:4–8

We will spend one more day focusing on Joshua's obedient circumcision of the men of Israel. Yesterday, we applauded the fact that there weren't even any questions recorded in this account. God said to circumcise and Joshua set about doing it. Today, we read that the Lord chose to provide His reason for this command even though no one demanded it.

Since the call of Abraham, Israelite men had been circumcised as a sign of covenant between God and man. In Genesis 15, God cut covenant with Abraham. If you look back at that passage of scripture, it is very obvious that covenant keeping was completely up to God. Abraham was no part of that agreement. In fact, God put him to sleep while He established details of the covenant. Later, in Genesis 17, God instructed Abraham to be circumcised and to circumcise Israelite men as a *sign* of the covenant. From the beginning, God's intention was to mark His people as different.

Abraham had children. His children had children. If you are part of a family that you'd describe as dysfunctional, you should really read through the latter part of Genesis. Abraham, God's chosen father, led a family full of dysfunction. Genesis ends when Joseph, Abrahams' great, great grandson, was established as a leader in Egypt. Through that, God saved His people from a wide spread famine. Between Genesis and Exodus, God's nation grew in number and strength, leading to fearful Egyptians abusing Hebrew slaves. God's people remained under Egyptian oppression for 400 years until God saw fit to draw them out. As you know, after the mighty and miraculous Red Sea parting, the Hebrews (Israelites) walked right back into the bondage of doubt and fear and wandered in the desert for forty more years. Are you seeing the theme?

God calls man into covenant.

Man accepts and commits but later fails and sin enslaves.

God rescues and redeems.

The whole cycle begins again.

Thank goodness we haven't been given the responsibility of upholding the covenant, because humanity has always failed. God only instructed that we be marked by the covenant. Old Testament marking was physical. It was real and permanent. During the forty years in the desert, though, circumcision wasn't practiced. Since God's people were preparing to go into their promised land, He determined they must bear the sign of His covenant *before* meeting opposition again. God knew the enemy would be great, so His people needed the physical reminder of their covenant with God. Although God would not forget the covenant He'd made with His people, the Israelites were prone to forgetfulness.

You know, I forget too. I can speak God's faithfulness in all situations then face opposition and crumble in a moment. I need to be *marked* by His covenant in a way that can't be forgotten. Often, like in circumcision, a wounding provides the mark needed to remember WHO I am because of WHO God is.

I've often focused on the sign of covenant being necessary to show *the world* my difference in Christ. In our Joshua passage, though, the enemy (the world) would NOT see the wounding of the circumcision. I believe God called the Israelite men to be circumcised prior to meeting their enemy to remind *them* of His faithfulness as a covenant-keeping God. We live New Testament lives where Old Testament law has been fulfilled. It is for freedom that Christ has set us free, so the laws of circumcision don't apply now. We are, however, called to be different, set apart, and marked by a relationship with God through Christ. How does that happen? What will it look like?

Simply put, a wounding makes us different. The causes are many and can be horrific, but the effects of a wounding given to God for healing are beautiful. An internal circumcision occurs when we allow a physical, relational, and emotional wounding to cut in a way that exposes our great need for a covenant keeping God who heals and restores. The pain of our difficulties forces us to focus on HIS ability and provides an experiential sign of God's active presence in our lives. Circumcision left a physical wounding and marking, but our trials leave marks of increased trust in God. While it's not outward, this inward sign makes us different in a way that others notice.

We can't celebrate pain, but we *can* and *we should* celebrate God's determination to be the ONE handling difficulties for us. Our job, according to Genesis 17, is to carry the sign of the covenant which is the Holy Spirit living in our hearts manifested in faith, trust, and obedience. Then, we can celebrate the future JOY that comes when we allow God to work in our wounding, causing us to grow in faith and trust in Him. Our inward and emotional sign of the covenant will move outward because active faith is evident! Others will see it and take notice. They will wonder where it comes from. They will want to know more about it. *Then,* we are given the pleasure of sharing covenant with the world! So, remember the wounding today. Give thanks for God's healing work and let it make you different. Your world *WILL* notice!

> *And not only this, but we also exult in our tribulations, knowing that tribulation brings about perseverance; and perseverance, proven character, and proven character, hope; and hope does not disappoint, because the love of God has been poured out within our hearts through the Holy Spirit who was given to us.* (Romans 5:3–5)

Day 15:
Live On Today's Provision!

Read Exodus 16 and Joshua 5:9–12

Today's narrative may read more like a journal entry than a devotion. I have so much on my mind concerning this scripture passage. Before I begin, I need to confess that I'll likely cry through most of my writing. God has used the concept of 'manna' to teach me rich truths about Himself and His love for me. Because of that, this point in Joshua's story is a sensitive one for me. When the manna—God's provision for the Israelites in the desert—ends, my heart feels the magnitude of it fully.

Have you ever experienced a season of wilderness wandering? I have. Just to be clear, I am speaking metaphorically. I've never even visited a true wilderness or desert. I don't have any experience there; if I did, it isn't likely I would come away with any great story to tell. However, I HAVE experienced the wilderness in the sense that, like the Israelites, I've lived in a season of wandering and searching. My husband and I know what it feels like to be on the move but not really sure of where to go or what to do. Nearly five years ago, Scotty's confession of adultery left him jobless and searching. With three children depending on us, we had to earnestly seek God's guidance; He was clear in moving us OUT of the land that we knew and INTO a land that was pretty foreign. Actually, it was only about three hours north and in the same state, but much of our new world was unknown. It was small town MS. I call it Mayberry.

Before I go on, I want you to know that I grew to *love* my new home, but it was my wilderness! Honestly, it wouldn't have mattered *where* God placed me at that point in my journey. After losing close friendships, comfort, and a million other things I couldn't even begin to name, I was due a season in the wilderness. In the beginning, I grumbled. Just like the Israelites in Exodus 16 and on, I didn't recognize God's provision in my experience. Did you know that the meaning for manna is "what is it"? Literally! When it fell to the ground, God's people didn't know what it was. They'd never seen it before. That was me in my new home. God provided a church home, new friends, a new career, and all the freshness that goes with those things. Yet, I grumbled at times because the provision wasn't recognizable.

It took some time, but Scotty and I plugged into our new community through our church, my gym, and some key friendships. We slowly found our place. While much of life still felt odd and a little uncomfortable, we began to recognize the *goodness* of the manna. God had provided new friends, new purpose in work, and new direction in ministry through this place I was sure would never feel like *home.* We'd begun to *appreciate* God's provision. At that point, I began to see the picture of manna in the desert as God's provision of HOPE against a backdrop of despair. He'd used a town full of people to do it.

You see, like the Israelites, Scotty and I were in a dark and heavy place during our wilderness wandering. We were like soldiers, wounded in battle and sent away to recover. Our marriage had been under attack and needed healing. As we were focused on that, the rest of life carried on at full speed: finances had to be managed, kids had to be raised, and jobs had to be completed. **Life was HARD!** Every single aspect seemed to require *all* we had. All around us, God was pouring down manna. He was sending us people and experiences that we *needed* in order to survive. Today, I can tell you I LOVE that small town in MS and all of its people. When the thought of that sweet place comes to mind, my heart smiles! We spent only four years there, but I will treasure it for the rest of my life. They were God's gift and provision to our family.

Then, God called us away. *The manna is seasonal.* If we aren't careful, we will allow our natural, human tendency to crave comfort, strapping us down until what God intended to be temporary provision becomes bondage. At some point, the manna will cease, because it's time to eat from new provision. Remember, in Exodus 16, the Israelites were given the specific instruction to gather only what they needed for that day. During the first days of manna, the struggle was trusting that it would actually arrive again the next day. The Israelites had to fight the daily urge to store up manna in case God didn't send it again. Throughout the wilderness journey, He did send it every morning. In Joshua 5, though, the Israelites observed the Passover, ate of the produce of the new land, and the manna ceased.

Ceased!

Rested!

Was put away!

For me, there is beauty, rejoicing, sadness, *and* grief in that word. Praise God for the picture of redemption He gives us in the Israelites. Even forty years in the desert didn't disqualify them from God's new purpose for their life. That gives me hope.

Knowing what I know about manna in my own life, though, I must also pause and grieve the loss for a moment. Now, when I think about manna, I actually see a church and its beautiful members along with sweet friends that encouraged us to carry on in difficult times. I hear crickets, birds, and other sounds of wildlife that inhabited the lake-side space that was ours in Mayberry for a short time. I feel the love and preciousness that small town MS holds for me. Through many tears, I say, "thank you, God, for the manna." Then, I trust Him for *today's* provision! When God initiated the new path for our family, we couldn't hold on to the old provision! It would have grown stale, and we would have done the same.

Did you notice in scripture that the Israelites actually ate from the goodness of Canaan AND THEN the manna ceased? Isn't our God a gracious God? I absolutely adore Him for the times in scripture where I see Him loving us so much that He gives us the confidence we need before calling us to exercise a little faith in a new calling. His people saw the fruit of Canaan, they actually ate some of it, *and then* the manna ceased.

Where are you? What goodness is God providing for you? Let's ask Him for wisdom to see and to know *His provision* for today and the faith to *live* fully and abundantly on it.

> *Open your mouth and taste, open your eyes and see—how good God is. Blessed are you who run to Him.* (Psalm 34:8, The Message)

Day 16:
Join God's Cause!

Read Joshua 5:13–15

h *ose side are you on?*
    Who's right and who's wrong?
Standing by Jericho, Joshua was confronted by a soldier with his sword drawn and these are the questions he asked him. Scripture doesn't say what Joshua was doing 'beside Jericho.' It just says that is where he was. I believe he was scoping out his next steps. Earlier in the chapter, the Israelite army was circumcised. They took time to heal, participated in the Passover, and ate from the produce of their promised land. I believe Joshua appeared by Jericho in today's reading because he was thinking through what could happen next. Joshua was facing enemy territory, looking at an armed soldier, and asking, "Whose side are you on?"

I've never been faced with armed enemies and the scary situations that might accompany those interactions. Being a believer, though, I am often faced with spiritual enemies. Frequently, I look into the faces (or posts) of people supporting beliefs and causes that are seriously opposed to my own. I have to decide how to respond. In many of those moments, I question whether God is for me or the other side in the disagreement.

As I'm writing this devotional, we are in presidential election season. On a daily basis, television, newspapers, and Facebook are filled with information on the candidates. Everybody has an opinion and perspective. That's understandable. What's discouraging for me is the tone of our believing community in handling the agreement. FEAR is driving slander and malice. It seems everyone feels their Christian beliefs justify the hateful tone. Isn't that ironic? I can't believe God is ever pro-slander, pro-hate, or pro-division.

God is for God! He just is. I find comfort in that. Our covenant-keeping God knows the beginning, middle, and end of every life, movement, and fight! He is *more than able* to bring about His plan through His followers AND His enemies. When Joshua asked the commander if he was for Israel *or* the enemy, the commander answered, "No!" Joshua must have been confused. It wasn't a *yes* or *no* question! He wasn't *for* Joshua's army OR the enemy. As the commander of the host of the Lord, He was *FOR GOD.* We should be, too.

We must *always* fight to uphold God's agenda and not our own. That's so hard to do when the world seems to have gone completely nuts. Fear takes over and it seems like goodness has possibly been lost forever. As the temple of the Holy Spirit, though, good and right aren't lost forever *in me!* My responses matter. I can choose to focus on that. In *My Utmost for His Highest,* Oswald Chambers says:

> "As Christians we are not out for our own cause at all, we are out for the cause of God, which can never be our cause. We do not know what God is after, but we have to maintain our relationship with Him

whatever happens. That (our relationship with Him) is all God asks us to look after, and it is the one thing that is being continually assailed."

We are called to be FOR God even without truly knowing what He is for at each step in the journey. No matter how hard I try to follow Jesus' example in this area, I continue to be confused by right and wrong in dealing with those who live differently than me. Oswald Chambers' quote states that my responsibility is to seek God in relationship. Joshua's response in Joshua 5:14 seems to fully agree:

> *And Joshua fell on his face to the earth, and bowed down and said to him, "What has my lord to say to his servant?"*

In difficult and trying times, believers are called to *HUMILITY!* Most of the time, we don't know what God is for because we can't hear His voice over our own noise. We desperately need to hear His voice. God will guide and direct in the area of personal responsibility. He will show us what to do, what to say, and how to respond. It will never contradict Himself. So, regardless of what the world around us looks like, we must act, speak, and respond in love, truth, and freedom. Always!

The commander of the Lord's army wasn't interested in telling Joshua *what* he was *against.* He made sure Joshua knew *who* he was *for!*

Since we are in an election year, let me clearly state that I'm not advocating Christians NOT state our beliefs and seek representatives that share them. I am saying that when the way seems dark and we can't find leaders to support that share our spiritual convictions, it's best to seek humility and focus on WHO we are for. He doesn't lose! He can't be stopped! He's very capable of using opposition to achieve His purposes. When fear threatens, faith must stand up and speak God's Truth in God's way!

God rules and reigns for all of eternity. Our lives can demonstrate the peace and joy that He offers by fighting the right battles and supporting the right cause. That battle will always be inward and the cause belongs to the Lord. How can you respond FOR Him today?

> *If My people who are called by My name humble themselves, pray and seek My face, and turn from their evil ways, then I will hear from heaven, forgive their sin, and heal their land.* (2 Chronicles 7:14)

Day 17:
See What God Sees!

Read Joshua 6

I hope some of you reading today are mothers who raised babies during the *Veggie Tales* era. If so, you can't read Joshua 6 without picturing tiny, talking vegetables walking around the wall of Jericho while other vegetables (peas in helmets I believe) mock and jeer from the wall. My boys LOVED "Josh & the Big Wall," and we watched it many times. My familiarity with the story doesn't make the content any easier to understand. How does a city wall crumble to the ground because of people circling, trumpets blaring, and voices shouting? How?

Before I get to that, though, I want to focus on verse two. The city of Jericho was tightly shut. No one came in and no one went out. Jericho's inhabitants were protected behind the wall. Yet, Joshua 6:2 says,

> *And the Lord said to Joshua, "See I have given Jericho into your hand with its king and the valiant warriors."*

If I were Joshua, I would have been very tempted to answer, "Um, No! Actually, I SEE a wall protecting a city that is definitely NOT in my hands."

God sees what we can't see. Sometimes, He asks us to *see* it, too. God didn't build Joshua up with a motivational speech. He didn't demolish the wall and invite Joshua to move in and take control. Clearly, Joshua had a work planned for him. First, though, God wanted him to *see* the victory of his calling.

One of the hardest things about marriage and parenting for Scotty and me is that we don't have a frame of reference for establishing unity in family. My parents divorced when I was very young, so I didn't have the opportunity to see them partner in life and family. I think that's why we've always been drawn to spending time with couples who are older and a little ahead of us in the process of raising children. We watch, ask for advice, and shamelessly copy.

A couple of years ago, we hit a rut in our marriage recovery, because we couldn't see a way out of our circumstances. For me, everything about life felt like we were going through the motions. It felt like we'd meandered back into survival, and I wanted to thrive. At that time, our oldest child was moving into teenage years, and no one was adjusting well. As an added bonus, we experienced a sharp disagreement with one of our parents and it rocked our family's world to the very core. We were still in counseling. I was participating in some individual therapy. I *knew* God wanted more for us. I understood He'd provide a way of relief from the pile up. I just couldn't *see* it yet.

Then, a few of our couple friends became grandparents. It was an amazing thing to watch. They absolutely loved it. Clearly, there was something precious about the experience. Their adventure allowed me to begin seeing what God wanted me to see. These friends had chosen to stick it out through the good and the bad. No doubt, they'd spent seasons in confusion like I was experiencing. Their angelic babies had probably turned into difficult teenagers. I'm sure there were times their marriages felt stale and dark. But, they partnered together. United, they allowed all of the difficult circumstances to provide maturity and growth in Christ. Their new stage of grand parenting almost seemed like a reward, a giant trophy at the end of a long, hard race, and the JOY was multiplied because they were sharing it *together.*

It was not my story, but God asked me to see it like it was. I began looking ahead to our children as adults, to grandchildren, and to the excitement of celebrating it all with Scotty. Obviously, the road to get there would continue to be rocky. There were going to be more highs and lows, but I realized that once we reach those milestones, the difficulties will have only served to bring about a sweeter celebration. Like Joshua, I needed to *see* the victory God had for us in order to persevere through the obstacles that were in front of us.

Then, the work of the Israelites demonstrated that it's necessary to fully OBEY God's plan to reach victory even if the way seems absurd. God's strategy for Israelite success—march around the city, blow the horns, carry the ark, go back every day for six days, march seven times on the seventh day, blow the horns and shout—was questionable. Joshua's response excluded any trace of question, however, because he saw what God saw. *His vision led to his obedience.*

Several months back, one of the friends I was speaking of earlier hugged my neck and said, "thank you for doing hard." It was a precious phrase and I will never forget it. She was thanking me for doing the right thing in my marriage even though it wasn't easy. What she didn't know is that God had used her simple enjoyment of a new grandbaby to encourage me. Because she persevered in marriage in a way that brought visible joy and fulfillment in the grandparent stage, I was able to *see* what God could have in store for me. That vision strengthened my obedience.

Can you see what God is preparing for you? If we could, don't you know we'd never even consider giving up? If you are having trouble with vision, ask God to give you a glimpse of His. Then, pursue that vision with hope and perseverance even if it feels like you're walking in circles. You may be one lap away from the obstacle crashing at your feet. Victory could be just one, crazy, obedient step away. Hang on, follow through, and don't give up!

> *Then the Lord answered me and said, "Record the vision and inscribe it on the tablets, that the one who reads it may run. For the vision is yet for the appointed time; it hastens toward the goal, and it will not fail. Though it tarries, wait for it; for it will certainly come, it will not delay"* (Habakkuk 2: 2–3 (NASB).

> *And then God answered: "Write this, write what you see. Write it out in big block letters so that it can be read on the run. This vision-message is a witness pointing to what's coming. It aches for the coming— it can hardly wait! And it doesn't lie. If it seems slow in coming wait. It's on its way. It will come right on time"* (Habakkuk 2: 2–3 (Message).

Day 18:
Praise God in Confession!

Read Joshua 7

I think it would be appropriate to begin today's devotion with a collective, "WOW!" Throughout our reading, the Israelites have experienced the power and presence of God in such a personal way. In chapter 6, we read about their obedience to follow God's somewhat odd battle plan which caused the wall of Jericho to crumble. We ended yesterday's study with victory, and today's chapter began in defeat:

> *But the sons of Israel acted unfaithfully in regard to the things under the ban (7:1).*

WHAT?!?!

If there was ever a time for God's people to stick closely to Him and follow His instruction *completely*, I think stepping into the Promised Land would be that time. They were living in the land God promised them and complete obedience to God's instruction had gotten them there. After such a long period of waiting, they were

SEEING promises fulfilled. Yet, sin entered the camp, so defeat was inevitable.

Achan sinned by taking what God had specifically asked him not to take, but it started with a simple look. The disobedience that caused Israel's defeat and cost Achan his life began with a glance towards something God had banned.

> *... when I saw among the spoil a beautiful mantle from Shinar and two hundred shekels of silver and a bar of gold fifty shekels in weight, then I coveted them and took them* (Joshua 7:21).

The simple explanation for Achan's sinful act is he *saw* something beautiful and *desired* it, so he *took* it. He *took* it! God had banned it, but Achan took it.

When you and I sin, we follow the same pattern. We reason that God is holding out on us, that what we *want* is better than what He *commands.* We fall for the same lie Adam and Eve believed in the Garden becoming convinced that our way is more profitable than His way. However, sin will never follow through with its promise to satisfy. Trapped by our sin, we will soon experience defeat, and others will be affected.

That is *always* sin's reality. It promises happiness, provision, and victory but delivers bondage, hiding, and defeat for *everyone* in the 'camp.' Personal sin affects corporate activity.

I'm somewhat of a night owl. I enjoy late night 'me' time. That's good, because my husband has always been early to bed. So, I put earbuds in my ears and watch a little Netflix before falling asleep. A couple of weeks ago, I felt God urging me to give up that time. I was deep in my study of Joshua, but I'd hit somewhat of a block in writing.

I felt God asking me to go on to bed each night without watching and rise a little earlier to study. I am ashamed to say that I thought the idea was ridiculous. Truly, I only watch about 20 to 30 minutes and then exhaustion takes over. What could it possibly hurt? So, for a little while I continued in my nighttime routine. The Lord stayed in my business, though, so I finally gave in! I turned in early with Scotty for several nights and before long I realized I was experiencing more depth in my study time each morning. I wouldn't have *said* I believed my ways were better than God's ways, but my actions for a little while demonstrated I must have. God had *banned* my Netflix time and I'd *taken* it anyway.

Sin!

God gave Joshua a plan to find the one who'd committed the sin that brought defeat upon Israel at Ai. Once he found him, Joshua had interesting advice for Achan:

> *My son, I implore you, give glory to the LORD, the God of Israel, and give praise to Him, and tell me now what you have done. Do not hide it from me* (Joshua 7:19).

Give praise?

Achan was guilty. Because of his sin, Israel had lost a battle in the Promised Land, but Joshua's advice was to *praise God* in full confession. Strange, isn't it? Confession wasn't going to bring back the men killed in battle. Coming clean wouldn't likely change the outcome of Achan's situation. So, **how could this act of confession also be an act of praise?**

I believe confession to be praise, because it acknowledges God's authority over *all* of life. Every time a hard heart and stubborn head choose fleshly desires over Godly direction, communication with our Heavenly Father is hindered. Destruction is the inescapable outcome. Yet, when we choose to humbly confess our personal weakness and repent, we turn back to face Him in humility which honors God as the authority.

That's WORSHIP!

Are you moving into new territory with God? Would you like to experience victory there? I would! The story of Achan demonstrates the necessity of full and complete obedience, but it also gives hope for our failures. God does not require perfection. He desires our praise. Confession is praise when it brings us face to face with God again through the power of Christ's redemption. Achan's end was decidedly near, but how gracious of God to let his final act be one of humility, praise, and honor! With a nation watching and an enemy gloating, Achan stepped forward and took responsibility for his sin.

Just as sin follows a pattern—see, desire, and take—I believe God answers sin with His own pattern of restoration; *uncover* sin in our life, *confess* it to Him in praise for His forgiveness, and *remove the sin* from our midst. Why hold on to that which destroys?

> *O Israel, You cannot stand before your enemies until you have removed the things under the ban from your mids.* (Joshua 7:13).

What has God 'banned' from your life? Are you hanging onto something or someone that He's asked you to give up? If God has spoken against it, remove it from your midst. He will not deliver the next set of instructions for your MOVE until the first set is obeyed. Be bold today and ask Him to uncover hidden sin in your midst. Then, be humble enough to praise Him in confession and allow Him to remove it.

In Hebrew, the word for "midst" in Joshua 7:13 is the same word as "within" in Psalm 51:10. I believe David's psalm of confession is a good place for us to begin praising God through confession. There's a reason God goes to the *center,* the *midst,* the *within* for the cleansing. **That's where He belongs**! So, let's put Him there today as we cry out to Him in confession's worship.

Create in me a clean heart, O God, and renew a steadfast spirit within me (Psalm 51:10).

Day 19:
Repeat God's Word!

I'm in over my head!
Have you ever had that feeling? By nature, I'm a perfectionist. I don't begin things I can't finish and finish well. But, I've initiated a project that I'm not sure how to finish. The project I'm referring to is what you are reading right now. Today, I cannot imagine how God is going to pull—no, *drag*—me to the end of this book. I'm not trained to write a book! When I hit a block or can't figure out how to personalize the next portion of scripture, I have to talk to myself. I have to repeat what I know to be true! In Philippians 1:6, God's Word says that He who started the work will complete the work. I have to remind myself (often OUT loud) that God gave me the vision to write *through* the book of Joshua with active trust that He will do it.

Read Joshua 8:1–2

DEFEAT! What do we do with defeat? It can absolutely paralyze. I wonder if the reality of recent failure in Ai and the fear of future failure caused Joshua to feel overwhelmed and *in over his head.* It appears that He did, because God began repeating Himself. In a crisis moment, when failure shattered confidence, sin required death, and defeat threatened calling, God simply *repeated* His earlier commands to Joshua.

Do you know that God's commands are for your good? Do you realize His great love *for* you causes Him to require full obedience *from* you? It's true! God's commands to us are to be followed if we want to live in the freedom a Promised Land provides. We've been given a choice. You and I can disregard God's instruction, but disobedience forfeits Promised Land living. In light of that truth, some commands are worth repeating;

- *FEAR NOT!* God reminded Joshua not to fear or be dismayed. In my personal opinion, he'd earned the right to fear. The Israelites, under Joshua's leading, *failed* miserably in their attempt to take Ai. No one would blame Joshua for *feeling* afraid. If he chose to *live* in fear, though, he could talk himself and his people out of God's plan for their future. So, what did God say?

  Do not fear or BE dismayed (8:1a)

  Joshua had to be reminded to control his feelings of fear and discouragement, or they would control him. He couldn't let defeat define him. You and I can't either. We have an assignment to fulfill! We are *moving* to new places with the Lord and failure will be part of the process. Hear God repeat His call to fearless living today and *kill* the discouragement. There's more to be done, and fear won't let you do it.

- *ARISE!* In a real crisis of belief, this is the command I have to repeat to myself most often. Writing this little devotional has tested my follow through on more than one occasion. Once fear begins to chip away at my determination to write, I want to lay down in defeat – *literally.* Rather than use my free time for writing, I want to nap, watch a movie, or sit and pout. When God's Word repeats in my ear I know I need to get up and do something. Even if I only pound out a couple of lines that later get deleted, the positive activity demolishes the negative thinking. God said:

Take all the people of war with you and arise, go up to Ai. (8:1)

No future plan of action was given. No details were highlighted to convince Joshua's obedience. God simply told him to get up and go. *Again.* We need that reminder too. Where are you headed with God? When the path is uncertain, every defeat can make us want to sit down and give up. I understand! But, we need to arise and do something. Take the next step no matter how little it may seem. Your activity will build confidence for another victory.

- *SEE WHAT GOD SEES!* Has God given you vision that has become cloudy with defeat? Our humanity is so frail and fragile. I have found that no vision can survive the depths of despair. Regardless of your journey, your battle, or your vision, God sees victory. His victory may look different than you pictured it would look, but He sees a WIN. If we are going to experience it, though, we have to see it *with* Him.

That's faith! It's also not something you can do on your own. When fear, discouragement, and defeat attack, you must ask God for His vision. I'm encouraging you to do it out loud! Cry out to God for sight. We don't have to see HOW it ends. We just need to see WHO wins. It's always, ALWAYS God through Jesus Christ.

> *but He, having offered one sacrifice for sins for all time sat down at the right hand of God waiting from that time onward until His enemies be made a footstool for His feet* (Hebrews 10:12–13).

Do you *see* it? Jesus *sat down,* because the victory had been won. Now, He waits for *all* enemies to fall for eternity. In the meantime, we can't live in fear. We get to rise up and overcome temporary defeats and fight for the vision God gave us.

Read Joshua 8:3–26

> *So Joshua rose with all the people of war to go up to Ai; and Joshua chose 30,000 valiant warriors, and sent them out at night. And he commanded them saying, "See you are going to ambush the city from behind it. Do not go very far from the city, but all of you be ready."* (Joshua 8:3–4).

Repeat God's commands when a reminder is necessary, then do the assignment. Make a plan, join forces with some valiant prayer warriors, and go! Do not quit until the full work has been done. I know you've endured failures before, because I have too! Those shortcomings can bring about debilitating panic *or* empowering focus. What did He say in the beginning of the journey that made you move towards new adventure with God? *It is STILL true!*

The failure and panic I've experienced in this writing process only mirror what I experience in life on a regular basis. Do you know why I've recently fallen to fear and dismay over finishing my writing? It's because I've written this particular entry and trashed it THREE times. Every time I highlight an entire section of writing and hit 'delete,' fear grips and threatens to take over.

I can't finish!

I'll never get to the end and create anything that will encourage, build up, or make a difference.

WHY did I even begin? What do I think I am going to do with a book anyway?

I could give countless examples of recurring marriage struggles, parenting fails, and emotional shortcomings that usher me into the same kind of conversation on a regular basis. You too? I thought so! What if TODAY we decide to move forward with focus? Could we choose to trust the responsibility of completion to the One who sees the end already and stands in triumph on our behalf?

You don't have to be afraid!

You can stand back up, brush yourself off, and begin again.

And, you can wait expectantly to see God do what only He can do through you AND your failures.

Then, as Joshua told the Israelites, BE READY, friend. My God does amazing things!

> *And Blessed is she who believed that there would be a fulfillment of what was spoken to her from the Lord* (Luke 1:45).

Day 20:
Obey Fully!

Read: Joshua 8:26–35

Today's reading will unfold more like a mini history lesson than a devotional. After following specific instructions and strategy, the Israelites defeated the people of Ai. At the end of that battle, Joshua had a lot to do and say. I believe we will gain more appreciation for his activity and words to the Israelites by looking back.

1. Joshua burned Ai, killed their king, and built an altar of uncut stones to the Lord. On those stones, he wrote a copy of the law of Moses (Joshua 8:30–32).

   And if you make an altar of stone for Me, you shall not build it of cut stones, for if you wield your tool on it, you will profane it (Exodus 20:25).

   So it shall be on the day when you shall cross the Jordan to the land which the LORD your God gives you, that you shall set up for yourself large stones, and coat them with lime

and write on them all the words of this law
(Deuteronomy 27:2–3).

2. Joshua and the people positioned themselves for
    the reading of the Law (Joshua 8:33).

    *And it shall come about, when the LORD your
    God brings you into the land where you are
    entering to possess it, that you shall place
    the blessing on Mount Gerizim and the curse
    on Mount Ebal* (Deuteronomy 11:29).

    *Moses also charged the people on that day,
    saying, "When you cross the Jordan, these
    shall stand on Mount Gerizim to bless the
    people; Simeon, Levi, Judah, Issachar, Joseph,
    and Benjamin. And for the curse, these shall
    stand on Mount Ebal: Reuben, Gad, Asher,
    Zebulun, Dan, and Naphtali."* (Deuteronomy
    27:11–13).

3. Joshua read the entire law, the blessing and the
    curse to the whole assembly of Israel (Joshua
    8: 35-36).

    *Assemble the people, the men and the
    women and children and the alien who is in
    your town, in order that they may hear and
    learn and fear the LORD your God, and be
    careful to observe all the words of this law*
    (Deuteronomy 31:12).

In simple terms, Joshua obeyed God completely!
Maybe he would have done this exact thing without the
loss at Ai. Possibly, he would have chosen to dot all I's and

cross all T's even if he'd not seen Achan, Achan's family, and their possessions burned and buried. However, I feel certain the losses helped to reinforce a determination to carry out all the Lord, through Moses, had commanded.

Maybe this whole scenario seems legalistic to you. If so, I completely understand. I really do, and I won't ask you to shift in that thinking! I'd rather you wrestle with God for yourself and find the answers you're looking for. I am going to ask you to consider the possibility that Joshua and the Israelites *had* shifted in their thinking. Isn't it possible that somewhere along the way they'd learned to obey God's Word completely, *because* they began to truly believe His way to be best? Could it be they'd seen enough blessings and curses to have learned (mostly the hard way) that God gives commands to keep His children safe?

I'm a rule follower by nature. Honestly, for as long as I can remember, I've simply been afraid to go against what I was told. But, I can't say I've always obeyed perfectly. I didn't necessarily follow God's rules out of a love and trust relationship with Him. I obeyed out of fear, dodging curses rather than seeking blessing.

After our marriage crashed in 2011, I began to look back and examine. There were many areas of my Christian walk that were compromised. I was playing it *safe!* God had been calling me to a life of full surrender, but instead I opted for neat and pretty. I didn't want to step out of my comfort zone and fight for His goodness in all areas of my life. I was obedient externally. But, inwardly, I rebelliously warred for my own way.

God can't honor *partial obedience,* because it doesn't lead to *fullness* in Christ. We are either in or we're out. We are FOR Him or AGAINST Him. By choosing to hold on to what I considered security, I'd forfeited His perfect protection. When life crashed around me, He was still faithful, but Scotty and I received consequences to remind us of our loving Parent.

I'm still a rule follower. Really, I just love boundaries, and I feel more comfortable within them. Now, though, I try to focus on internal boundaries. I know now what it feels like to live outside the walls of safety with God. I've learned, by experience, that His commands for me and invitations to me are for my good even if they take me outside of comfortable. I'm still fearful of disobeying but, instead of fearing the curse, I fear missing the blessing.

I believe the fullness of the Israelites' obedience in today's chapter beautifully illustrates their understanding of God's heart towards them. Their unbroken obedience was a declaration of faith in a trustworthy God. I pray daily that God builds belief in me that always chooses blessing over curse and life over death. He's the only safeguard we need to follow through and move forward well.

> *See, I have set before you today life and prosperity, and death and adversity; in that I command you today to love the LORD your God, to walk in His ways and to keep His commandments and His statutes and His judgments, that you may live and multiply, and that the LORD your God may bless you in the land where you are entering to possess it* (Deuteronomy 30:15–16).

Day 21
Ask God About . . . Everything!

Read Joshua 9:1–16

There are times during my Bible reading that I need to switch from my New American Standard version and read The Message. In verse fourteen, Eugene Peterson translates, "The men of Israel looked them (the Gibeonites) over and accepted the evidence. But, they didn't ask God about it." I've read that last part over and over, and I have only one question.

Why?

There's nothing judgmental about my question. My 'why' comes from a place of pure curiosity. Why didn't Joshua and the men of Israel consult God about something as serious as making a covenant with foreign people? My curiosity grows exponentially when I reflect on the fact that every move, up until this point, had been made after carefully seeking the Lord's guidance and following through with clear determination. Here, though, Joshua encountered a wandering group of people, asking for an agreement that would ensure safety through a relationship, and he agreed to their terms without conferring with God.

Did Joshua feel like helping a weaker nation was the right thing to do? Could he have felt that turning away from people begging for help couldn't have been the good decision for God's people? If so, I've certainly been there. In fact, on more occasions than I can count, I've gotten myself into upsetting circumstances because I chose the *kind* response without asking God to help me discern the *best* response.

Possibly, Joshua and the leaders in Israel simply had their minds FULL with other decisions to be made and felt the decision with the Gibeonites could be made quickly. They'd just finished fighting several battles and they knew more were coming. Maybe they needed to get back to strategic planning, so they hurried a covenant decision in order to quiet the nagging and move on. I'm remembering a few times when I made quick decisions in seemingly minute situations, because huge decisions in situations of magnitude were looming. Apparently, small choices can lead to giant consequences when made without God's guidance.

I could be reading too much into the whole scenario and Joshua simply trusted his own common sense. What could it hurt to help a needy group of people? Besides, the covenant would definitely pack more people on Israel's side.

At moments like these, I really wish I had some seminary knowledge to share. I'm just a mom and former school teacher with a curious mind to search God's Word for wisdom that applies to life. The obvious truth of this passage is that no decision should be made without asking God for help, guidance, and supervision. I know God is sovereign! He *allowed* Joshua to be duped by the Gibeonites, so He was planning to use it for His glory and their good.

If Joshua had consulted Him, He may have actually been in favor of the covenant. However, when the Israelites face the battle we will look at tomorrow, I imagine they would much rather have been SURE they were fighting a battle God had ordained.

One of the most frustrating feelings I've endured in the healing process of the past five years is the inability, at times, to make decisions. Sometimes, simple choices reveal that I'm paralyzed by a lack of trust in myself. I don't know when this happened or why it happened. I just noticed a pattern of fear in decision making as God began leading us out of the heaviness that was our life during the early days of healing and into new areas of life and ministry. My brain has been experiencing "newness overload." Internally and externally, facing decisions I've never faced before, every choice becomes an opportunity to doubt, stress, and overthink. It's exhausting! And, it's downright annoying to feel unable to choose wisely in a sea of options.

For me, uncertainty and indecisiveness have been extra helpful in driving me right back to God. Honestly, I *need* to be somewhat fearful of the decisions I'd make for myself. One blessing of God calling me to MOVE forward with Him into new territory is that I've been forced to ask for His help even in the tiniest of choices. When everything around me is new, different, and unknown, I must have the wisdom of God before I can confidently step forward. There is such thing as a healthy fear that reinforces our great need for Christ in every earthly encounter.

What decisions are you facing today?

Who's asking you for an alliance?

Seek the Lord's guidance. Ask God about it. Do not make your choice without the counsel of God. Then, wait for His answer. I believe God is faithful to answer His children. Why would He tell us to come to Him and then refuse to give us an answer when we do? Once we've asked, though, we have to listen for the quiet response. Often, God has answered my pleas for guidance in ways that still call for an active faith and trust.

When Scotty and I were positive God was calling us back into ministry and that it would likely require a move to Florida, we had MANY decisions to make. MANY! I won't list them all, but finding a school for our children was a priority and an urgent decision for me. All three of our children had been homeschooled, but God had clearly shown us it was time for them to return to a school setting. I was going to have to make a decision about their school from eleven hours away without knowing anything about Florida's education system. Because we didn't want to limit our search for a home by the school in each district, we were given the names of a couple of private schools. I jumped online immediately and visited the sites. As I read through the information on the first site I found, a peace rushed over me that I cannot adequately describe. Several weeks later, we were able to visit this school. As we walked through the campus, met teachers, and observed students, I experienced a calming of my Spirit. I did not *feel* or *hear* God saying, "This is the school for Caleb, Collin, and Claire." But, I felt peace.

As we were packing up our house and making final arrangements for the move, I got a phone call that the other private school had some teacher openings. It was recommended that I apply there. Now, I suppose I should insert that private school tuition was NOT in the budget for our family. We were actively trusting God in a BIG way for provision. So, the recommendation to apply to teach at another school was tempting! It was the hope of some income and a price break in tuition. I was so torn! I felt peace about the first school we visited, BUT, common sense and basic math reasoned I should at least investigate the possibility of a job.

Several days later, I called my sister to update her on all that was going on. I briefly explained my school dilemma. With a million decisions to be made, I thought school was taken care of. My mind was racing and I had no idea how to make the right decision. Very calmly, she said, "Our God is a God of peace. When He gives it, we follow it." I followed peace and I've had confidence in our school decision since that moment. God has faithfully assured me more than once that peace in the midst of our school search was His guidance for that decision.

Maybe it seems I've gotten off track today. I'll admit that I've swerved a little from our text. Here's where I'm going, though. Joshua and the men of Israel asked a very good question of the Gibeonites multiple times. Basically, they said, "How can we be sure that you are who you say you are?" Because the question was repeated, I don't believe anyone felt peaceful about an alliance with the Gibeonites.

I want to ask you to write out some questions you have for God. Make a list of decisions you have to make and include ALL of your decisions. You may have some HUGE questions for God. If you're journeying to a place of NEW, most likely there are some areas where you are in desperate need of God's instruction. Take those questions to God, but don't miss out on the opportunity to receive guidance in your small, everyday decisions as well.

Jesus lived a perfect life on Earth. Over and over, He gives the answer for HOW He operated in perfection.

> *So Jesus explained, 'I tell you the truth, the Son can do nothing by himself. He does only what he sees the Father doing. Whatever the Father does, the Son also does' (John 5:19).*

If Jesus, being fully God, watched His Father and relied completely on Him to live, act, and work here on Earth, we certainly must do the same. Consult the Lord about everything! Wait for Him to answer. Apart from Him, we can do nothing except make a big, giant, mess.

Day 22:
Practice Integrity in Relationships

Read Joshua 9:17–10:11

My Joshua study has been paused for the past few days because I had the privilege of sitting under Beth Moore as she taught from the book of Proverbs. For three sessions, we studied the topic of WISDOM. To begin the conference, Beth asked us (all 9,000 of us) to recall a time God's wisdom was given. Proverbs teaches emphatically that *all* wisdom comes from God, but sometimes He supplies the perfect answer at the perfect time. It is obvious HE alone is the provider.

When I was in college, I dealt with some questions and frustrations over my parents' divorce. My parents divorced when I was ten years old, so when I began to struggle with certain aspects of my divided family as a sophomore and junior in college, I didn't understand the timing. One particular day, I was sitting in my car in the movie theater parking lot waiting on a group of friends. I was feeling helpless and hopeless concerning my family's dysfunction. I wasn't seeking God for His guidance at that moment. I was MAD about facing the family struggles again, and I was pitying myself for having to consistently deal with the consequences of decisions I didn't make. The Lord spoke a word over me that day that I haven't been able to shake since. He didn't speak audibly, but it felt so real to me. I felt the Lord say:

> You *are not* responsible for the choices and decisions other people have made that affected you. You most certainly *are* responsible for your responses to them. *Honor your father and your mother that your days may be long in the land which the LORD your God gives you.*

Honestly, my initial response to this piece of instruction made me angry at God. So, there I sat in my Plymouth Acclaim *mad at parents* and *mad at God.* **But, not for long.** As He's always faithful to do, the Lord quickly helped me to see that His wisdom always breathes LIFE and HOPE into frustrating circumstances. His wisdom gave me something I could do when I felt like a victim in a sad situation. I could focus on my responsibility to respond well.

How wise is our God that He'd take the time to teach me that lesson sixteen years before I'd need to have it cemented into the fiber of my being! When Scotty confessed his adultery to me, you better believe I was angry and hurt. Trust me when I tell you that I threw myself more than one pity party and plotted ways he could pay for my pain and embarrassment. However, God gently reminded me of His lesson concerning personal responsibility. Scotty had sinned and His sin created consequence for me, but his sin wouldn't justify a sinful response from me.

Joshua may have received the same lesson in personal responsibility in today's reading. When the people of Gibeon came to Joshua demanding protection from an enemy made up of five nations, Joshua could have said, "You lied to us. You tricked us into covenant with you. Therefore, we aren't responsible for you. You're on your own."

If Joshua's focus had been Gibeonite deceit, he could have said all of those things, but Joshua demonstrated a committed integrity. So, rather than look for a way *out of* the covenant with the Gibeonites, Joshua looked for a way to honor it and God honored him! Joshua and all his valiant men went to battle. God confounded the enemy to give Israel the advantage. Then, He sent hailstones to do even more damage than the soldiers did.

Five years ago, I could have walked away from the vows I made to my husband. There are verses in the New Testament that gave me permission. To many people, believers included, Scotty broke his vows which allowed me to break mine. Yet, I believed with all of my heart I would have missed God's **best** for me if I had chosen the way *out.* I'm even more convinced of that truth today. The world is looking for ways to get out of commitments. Believers should be looking for ways to remain strong in covenant, *because* God continues to honor covenant with us.

If you stop for a moment and think about it, I bet you are surrounded by troubled situations caused by someone stepping out of a position they agreed to hold. With seemingly good reasons to back up the decision, husbands are leaving wives, moms aren't mothering, friends aren't being friendly, employees aren't doing their jobs, and this list could go on and on. I'm convinced that we can't independently move forward with God towards abundant life without allowing God to sanctify us through relationships. Sometimes, we need to stay in relationship with difficult people to realize how desperate we are for Christ's intervention on a regular basis.

Look again at the message the men of Gibeon brought Joshua:

> *Do not abandon your servants; come up to us quickly and save us and help us, for all the kings of the Amorites that live in the hill country have assembled against us* (Joshua 10:6).

Don't you know Joshua wanted to answer harshly! I imagine something within him wanted to remind the men of Gibeon that he'd made a covenant not to kill them, but he'd said nothing about stepping back and allowing them to *be* killed.

Regardless of what he wanted to say, Joshua rallied his men and they went to battle. Maybe he didn't want to uphold his end of the bargain with the deceptive Gibeonites, but the Israelites showed up and demonstrated integrity. They committed to the battle and let God do the fighting.

That word, *abandon*, is used in several scriptures, but in Deuteronomy 4:31 it's used in a similar manner:

> *For the LORD your God is a compassionate God; He will not fail you nor destroy you nor forget the covenant with your fathers which He swore to them.*

Do you think it's possible Joshua remembered Moses speaking these words? Abandon and fail are the same word, *raphah.* Maybe Joshua was recounting Israel's dishonesty with God while remembering that He'd never chosen to abandon His covenant with His people.

I believe we need to renew our commitment to **integrity** in relationships. Our world has moved so far from the perfect world in the Garden of Eden. We are many, many, MANY generations beyond man's perfection in Adam. Sin has multiplied so many times that it's hard to imagine how much longer the Lord will tarry. Therefore, we are broken people trying to relate to one another. Often, it's just easier to step out, start over, and move on.

Having integrity, though, means we do what we said we'd do even when we don't feel like DOING it anymore. We will never fully live God's abundant plan for our lives if we keep stepping away from the people He's called us to live it with.

I know it's hard!

I realize it's isn't always fun!

I understand you don't see how to *remain* in relationship with someone who exposes all of your weaknesses.

And that's exactly the point. Let the difficulty uncover weakness, because then God can send the hailstones and obliterate the *real* enemy. Stay in the battle, but let God do the fighting. He's better at it anyway.

Don't you think we'd have a greater impact on this world and the people we live with if we were committed to integrity in our relationships? Establish healthy boundaries. Seek wise counsel when needed. Approach every offense with a determination to honor covenant, to stay IN the fight rather than to search for the way OUT. It just might be the key to fulfilling the abundant joy of your calling.

> *Don't hit back, discover beauty in everyone.*
> *If you've got it in you, get along with every-*
> *body. Don't insist on getting even; that's not*
> *for you to do. "I'll do the judging," says God.*
> *"I'll take care of it." Our scripture tells us that*

if you see your enemy hungry, go buy that person lunch, or if he's thirsty, get him a drink. Your generosity will surprise him with goodness. Don't let evil get the best of you; get the best of evil by doing good (Romans 12:17–21, *The Message*).

Day 23:
Pray CrAzY Prayers

Read Joshua 10:12–43

God is simply amazing! His care and concern for my little life baffle me. At this point in my Joshua study, I get to write about an ongoing topic of my questioning over the past few years. As I've wrestled with God in curiosity, He's been gracious to teach through people, books, and His Word. Sometimes, the voices of this world (even well-known and intelligent voices) distract me. In those times, I have to separate myself from the noise to seek my all-knowing God, and He is always faithful to speak clearly through His Word. This morning, I've realized my struggling and wrestling has equipped me to write *this* devotional *for you.* He is so smart!

I grew up in a Christian home and have always been a member of a Bible-believing church. I'm thankful for it. No family or church is perfect, but my life has been positively shaped by the spiritual teaching I received in both. I've also been negatively affected by the judgmental conversations in Christian circles. Phrases like "new age theology" and "prosperity gospel" have created *fear* in my thought processes. A few years ago, God began to push me to think for myself. He encouraged me to wade into seas of uncertainty with Him as the guide. I found that He can be trusted to keep me grounded in faith while searching for His Truth. Until that point, I had never felt free to explore my beliefs.

Then, Scotty and I hit a point in marriage and family recovery that was harder than hard. The rebuilding part would have been manageable if every other aspect of life could have been set to auto pilot. However, work and businesses still needed constant attention and that was draining. Our children continued to move into new life stages and that was challenging. Ongoing relation-ship strains nipped at our heels and that was frustrating. Life didn't stop just because we'd determined we would stay married and fight for our family. We grew weary in our fight.

I can't be sure, but I feel like Joshua may have been feeling some of that same stress. In the middle of his bat-tlefield, when the enemy had been slain by swords and pummeled by hailstones yet continued to fight, Joshua cried out to the Lord for *the sun to stand still*. What a bizarre prayer! Wouldn't it have been safe just to ask for guidance, strength, and wisdom to win and move on?

Apparently, Joshua wasn't interested in *safe*. Friends, I don't think we should be either! We are in a war! Right now, in the middle of our journey through Joshua, God may be showing you a calling, a path, or a way to walk with Him into something new. All throughout that path, there will be obstacles. What should we do about those? I'm just being honest in my wrestling, but how do we move forward when God gives direction and then leaves hurdles in the path?

I can only tell you what I plan to do. I will PRAY!

If that last sentence didn't send chills down your spine while a hearty "YES!" erupted from your mouth, you *may* be praying safe prayers. Throughout the New Testament, Jesus taught that He answers prayers according to the faith of the one praying. Joshua had enormous faith and it changed science. Somehow, the sun stood still!

> *O sun stand still at Gibeon and O moon in the valley of Aijalon. So the sun stood still, and the moon stopped, until the nation avenged themselves of their enemies* (Joshua 10:12–13).

Joshua's prayer sounds like an order! He was bold enough to cry out to God and ask for Him to rearrange the course of a day, to stop the Earth's movement around the sun, so that the day could last *until* the enemy was defeated. Wasn't God offended at Joshua telling Him what to do? God organized the sun, moon, and stars in the beginning. Certainly, He wasn't going to upset His plan just because Joshua asked for it!

Except that's exactly what He did!

Honestly, I can't imagine what would have possessed Joshua to pray for the sun to stand still! Why wouldn't he ask for more of the hailstones? I would have asked for the enemy to experience a collective heart attack. You know, "if every soldier could somehow just drop in his tracks, God, that would be awesome!" I would want God to intervene *before* any more fighting was necessary. Joshua didn't ask for deliverance or strength. He asked for *more time* to do what they'd already been doing. So, God gave it to him.

As I've prayed, searched, and read to figure out what God wants from me in prayer, I've come to the conclusion that He just wants me to believe Him and ask. In my spirit, I have the feeling He enjoys crazy and impossible prayers.

I find confidence in trusting God as my heavenly Father, and I trust that He answers prayer for a couple of reasons.

First, God is the One that calls us into prayer. The urge to pray for a situation is a burden placed in our hearts by God. When I feel the gentle nudge to pray, I ask Him to guide me in praying. Then, I trust that He will be victorious in that situation. My God is believable. He is sovereign over this world and all that is in it. So, I claim victory in His name.

Secondly, God's ways are perfect and I acknowledge that in prayer. Currently, Scotty and I are praying over a fairly large financial situation. We are in a bit of a mess. Like Joshua fighting the Gibeonites' battle, our mess is the making of our own doing. I am praying for God's favor over our finances. I'm praying for abundant provision and deliverance from all debt. I'm speaking it and claiming victory in Jesus' name *while* I confess that God's ways are higher than my ways. In humility, I'm assured that however God chooses to answer, His victory is better than mine. I choose HIS prosperity because His determination of good is best!

I believe God's people need to start praying wild and crazy prayers, because we serve a God that performs miracles. He crumbles city walls, sends hailstorms to kill enemies, and makes the sun stand still in the sky. He heals the sick and raises the dead. He leaves tombs empty for goodness sakes!

Where do you need enemies to fall instantly or time to stand still while you fight harder? *Ask for it!*

Is there something dead that needs to live again? *Ask for it!*

Have you given up hope that you can be delivered from your fears, bondage, addiction, debt, or difficulty? *Ask for your freedom!*

Right now, I'm going to hit my knees. I will take every burden I have before the Lord with boldness and audacity. What about you? Are you ready to take the obstacles to the Lord and trust He knows what to do with them? God can be trusted to work out *all things* for good. We either believe that or we don't. I want you to believe Him all the way to abundance in every area of your life. He is the reward, the very great reward, and we'll find Him in our asking!

> *Behold, I am the LORD, the God of all flesh; is anything too difficult for Me?* (Jeremiah 32:27)

> *Jesus said to them, "With men this is impossible, but with God all things are possible."* (Matthew 19:26)

Day 24:
Persevere in the LONG Battle!

Read Joshua 10:29–43 and 11

Today's scripture passage is lengthy, but I NEED for you to read it entirely. If you skimmed or skipped, please go back and read. I promise I'll try and make my writing shorter today. It's extremely important to me that you read God's Word. I'm happy He's asked me to share some of my story as we go, but I want to be sure that His message (more than mine) is the backbone of your study. We have seven days of study left and over ten chapters of Joshua still to cover. Our daily reading may become longer, but please commit to it. When we reach the end, I want us to have read the entire book.

Can you count the number of battles Joshua and the Israelites fought in northern and southern Palestine? I'm just going to be honest, I tried and kept losing my place. (Check out chapter 12, because the exact number of kings utterly destroyed by the Israelites is listed.) After praying his crazy prayer, Joshua drug five kings out of a cave, slaughtered them, and hung them for all to see. Amazing! God's power was put on display for anyone willing to look.

There had been one battle after another since the wall of Jericho crumbled to the ground. Once the sun stood still and five kings were defeated and hung, surely Israel's warriors would gain peace in the Promised Land.

Joshua and the Israelites still had more fighting to do. Since I promised you short commentary, I want to jump right to the point of today's lesson for me. *Sometimes the right battle is the long and hard battle!* I've sometimes been quick to assume I've made a wrong choice, followed an incorrect lead, or simply made a mistake when difficulty lingers. I judge the correctness of my position by the size of the opposition. If Joshua thought like I often do, he would have stopped fighting early on and retraced his steps back to the Jordan to seek a different path or at least an easier way.

Where would I have learned that the right journey should be simple? Wherever the idea came from, I'm convinced it is wrong! There is no easy or pretty route here on earth. Our lives will be hard and battles will carry on without obvious solutions. When one trial ends, the next one may be waiting to attack. No matter the difficulty, our call is to completion and we *need* perseverance!

In my circle of relationships, I know of difficult marriages, financial struggles, infertility wounds, uncertain adoptions, and broken communication. Really, that just scratches the surface. In each of these situations, the main frustration is that the hardship persists. Human weakness desires a fix, because life would be so much easier if the trouble would just end. I believe God isn't concerned with simple as much as He is in sanctification.

The ongoing battles could be the tool to bring about true cleansing and healing in our lives. Continuous struggles might be our ticket to a deeper relationship with the Lord. My journals are full of prayers begging for deliverance from unrelenting hardships. At times, I'd celebrate a win and hope it meant arrival at the final victory only to struggle *again* down the road. I became completely frustrated with the Lord. Like a spoiled child, I ranted with Him about the continuous nature of my battles. I acknowledged that He *could* make the battle end and questioned *why* He didn't. With a word, God could have given me an ultimate victory.

He didn't, however, so I pouted. I pointed at others who seemed to have an easier life. I was mad, and I didn't care that God knew it. I wasn't bailing on God or looking elsewhere for answers. He was God, and I was afraid to leave Him. I just felt hurt and mistreated.

Do you know what our all-gracious, all-knowing, and very loving Father did? He let me pout! That made me even angrier. He also held on and never let me quit, so I learned to trust Him even more. He taught me that difficulty doesn't necessarily equal mistake. Difficulty just equals LIFE!

Perseverance could be our most necessary asset as believers. Like Joshua, we need to be willing to wage war against the Enemy for as long as it takes to be able to say at the end of it all, *we've left nothing undone of all that the LORD had commanded* (Joshua 11:15).

Whatever your struggle is, name it with the Lord. If you've been fighting the battle for a long time and feel as if maybe God has forgotten about you, be honest with Him in those feelings. As long as you're wrestling with the Lord, you're still in the fight. Paul says:

> *And not only this, but we also exult in our tribulations, knowing that tribulation brings about perseverance; and perseverance, proven character, and proven character, hope, and hope does not disappoint, because the love of God has been poured out*

within our hearts through the Holy Spirit who was given to us (Romans 5:3–5).

Fight long and hard, friend! Your Enemy will be utterly defeated! In the meantime, allow the ongoing struggle to sanctify. No matter how long it takes, God *will* complete His promises to you.

Now, may the God of peace Himself sanctify you entirely, and may your spirit and soul and body be preserved complete without blame at the coming of our Lord Jesus Christ. Faithful is the One who calls you, and He will bring it to pass (1 Thessalonians 5:24).

Day 25:
Set Boundaries!

Read Joshua 17

We've skipped a few chapters in our reading today. Chapters 13 through 19 of Joshua contain instruction for dividing the Promised Land. In total, Joshua had led God's people to victory over 31 kings, and it was time for Israel to receive the land God promised. Establishing boundary lines was a necessary step in Joshua's obedience to God in the process of moving into the Promised Land.

I'm actually writing this entry after finishing all of Joshua. Originally, I planned to skip over these chapters only mentioning the division of the land. Today, as I was working on something else, it occurred to me that setting boundaries is monumentally important in a transition. I'm not familiar with the land Joshua was naming, but I am very familiar with new responsibilities in new seasons of life.

Very early in the healing of our marriage, God led me to write openly and publicly about our experiences in my blog. Not many people followed me. I'd really set it up as a way to share pictures and stories of our children for family that lived away. Honestly, that's when I first discovered a love for writing. I'm not typically the one to speak up in public settings, so writing my thoughts and feelings was liberating. Then, I realized I could formulate mini devotionals with each blog post to go with pictures I was sharing. I was able to flaunt precious pictures of my children along with beautiful lessons from the Lord. I was hooked!

Shortly after Scotty confessed his adultery to me, I unplugged from all social media. I deactivated my Facebook account and tried to forget about the blog. Only a couple of weeks later, I logged back into my dashboard. Processing life's trials via writing had become my outlet and freedom. More than ever, I needed to get back to the keyboard and analyze my thoughts and feelings with the Lord. So, I wrote about the beauty of God's power in the midst of adultery's ugliness! A couple of years into our healing, friends and friends of friends began sending messages my way. They all sounded something like this,

> Hey! I've been reading your blog, and my husband and I are going through a similar process. I was wondering if we could talk.

I can't even begin to describe the energy I felt from those messages. There was no way to celebrate the events that brought these people to me, but I *did* celebrate the fact that I'd been equipped to help. I was all in! During the summer of 2014, FOUR women contacted me. I felt honored, humbled, and *overwhelmed*, but I went to work and felt the need to be completely available to these women in their crises. When they messaged, I dropped everything to answer. During my personal quiet time, I thought about them and their marriages. I brainstormed ways I could help. I allowed my thought life to consider their situations regularly, which naturally took me back to the details of my own story. It was too much, so I needed boundary lines. Eventually, I set some but not before the heaviness of it all nearly buried me in heavy emotion.

Coming out of a wilderness season into a season of renewed purpose is exciting! The lessons I learned in the desert of adultery's pain created a passion that began to drive my ministry calling. I've always had a desire to serve women by teaching God's Word. That interest was multiplied because of my experiences. During the summer of 2014, I let zeal direct my path leaving no room for margin. Physically, I was spent. Emotionally, I felt drained. No amount of passion can fuel ministry in that condition. I was forced to step back and reevaluate. Boundaries are the necessary protection for you *and* those you serve.

Joshua says:

> *For though it is a forest, you shall clear it, and to its farthest borders it shall be yours; for you shall drive out the Canaanites, even though they have chariots of iron and though they are strong* (Joshua 17:18).

There's a fine line between establishing boundaries and becoming complacent. When God gives passion, we must be willing to put it to work, but seeking Him in the process is necessary. Here, in the book of Joshua, the men of Manasseh needed more land because God had given them so much victory. What great news! The answer to their land issue would require more work. That is always the case! We must set up and protect boundaries because we *will* fight more battles.

As a therapist, Scotty knew that many marriages healing from adultery end in the second year. That was so strange for me to hear early on. It just seemed like once a couple had given two years to the process, they'd surely just stick it out. Once we'd completed our second year, I understood that's where many people call it quits because that's when reality sets in that marriage could always be hard. It will always be work. The tribe of Manasseh had experienced victories and that was awesome. Those victories created a need and they had to work for the provision. The land was there, but it had to be cleared.

Since each victory might create the need for another battle, we better establish boundaries to protect our strength, our vision, and our purpose. I believe tomorrow's devotion will offer more detail in how to do this. Today, I felt we should recognize Joshua's charge to set up boundaries as the Israelites entered their Promised Land, because boundary lines are just as crucial for us. What a shame it would be to step into a new territory of passion and purpose without establishing limits to guard the strength we'll need for upkeep! God will finish what He started, friend. He will establish our boundaries, and they'll forever be growing when we are careful to seek Him in the process.

> *The LORD is the portion of my inheritance and my cup; Thou dost support my lot. The lines have fallen to me in pleasant places; Indeed, my heritage is beautiful to me. I will bless the LORD who has counseled me; Indeed, my mind instructs me in the night.*
>
> *I have set the LORD continually before me; Because He is at my right hand, I will not be shaken. Therefore, my heart is glad, and my glory rejoices; My flesh also will dwell securely.* (Psalm 16:5–9)

Day 26:
Establish a Place of Refuge!

Read Joshua 20

I really must begin with the fact that, at first glance, today's reading has *absolutely nothing* to apply to our lives. The Israelites took possession of their land and established six cities of refuge for *unintentional murderers!* I have a hard time with that. I'm not saying that I *never* mess up or sin without intention, but murder?

> *You have heard that the ancients were told, 'You shall not commit murder' and 'Whoever commits murder shall be liable to the court.' But, I say to you that everyone who is angry with his brother shall be guilty before the court and whoever shall say to his brother, 'Raca' shall be guilty before the supreme court; and whoever shall say, 'You fool,' shall be guilty enough to go into fiery hell* (Matthew 5:21–22).

If I focus on the fact that Joshua was establishing a safe place for a murderer to hide, I have great difficulty applying it to my life. When I trade out 'murder' for 'sin,' the application is clearer. The cities of refuge were set up to protect the offender from the offended. The sinner was removed from camp to provide security from a retaliator. I wonder if a secondary purpose was to give the sinner an opportunity to reflect. All sin, even unintentional sin, has a cause. We are very wise to make space in our lives so that God can uncover the root of our own sin and bring about personal change.

For the purpose of this study and application of this lesson in our lives, I want to use the cities of refuge as an illustration for our daily quiet times. Throughout my teenage and young adult years, I consistently heard messages on the importance of spending time with God daily. I attempted to make it a priority. After Scotty's confession, my quiet time became my salvation. I needed that time like I needed air to breathe. I began to set my alarm clock earlier than I'd ever woken before. I would open my Bible, pray, and journal like my life depended on it; I mostly believed that it did. In my pain, I needed to be protected from others and they needed to be protected from me. During my early morning quiet time, I felt the safety Joshua ordered the unintentional sinner to have in the cities of refuge.

Very quickly, though, I realized something else was happening in that quiet, safe place of meeting with God. In the space that God and I had originally created to hide me in his protection while I healed from the hurt and pain caused by others, He asked me to start dealing with areas in my own life that could lead me to sin (even unintentionally) against someone else. As I was pleading with God to change many of *my circumstances,* He was gently changing *me.*

*Search me, O God, and know my heart; Try
me and know my anxious thoughts; And see if
there be any hurtful way in me, and lead me
in the everlasting way* (Psalm 139:23–24).

Turn this scripture into a prayer and you have an awesome way to begin a quiet time. I love praying it because it gives God permission to show me sin that I don't see. When I pray this prayer, I'm asking God to change *my* heart. I believe He loves to honor that prayer. See, I can never control my circumstances. I'll never be able to force another person in my life to shift their behavior, but **I have the power to change myself.** When life goes crazy, sin hurts, or everything feels out of control, I can go to a place of refuge with God and give Him permission to search *my* heart and expose *my* sin. Since the blood of Christ covers *all* sin, it only holds the power to continue hurting when we refuse to see it, repent, and follow Him into the everlasting way.

I have a great friend and mentor that has guided me in so many of life's stages. I first met her when I started babysitting her children as a college student. When the first of those children was a young adult, they experienced difficulty in their relationship. When the pain in the relationship became impossible to overcome, my very wise friend searched for a Christian counselor. Their time in therapy was grueling. They covered some difficult topics. I didn't hear about all of it by any means, but what I did hear was tough to understand. From my perspective, the daughter's arguments against her mother were false. By all accounts, my friend is one of the best mothers I've known, and her daughter seemed to be refusing to see it. I was offended *for* my friend. She willingly went to session after session and looked for her own sin (even unintentional) that was hindering relationship. She wasn't too afraid or too prideful to admit fault, and, at the end of it all, she and her daughter were closer. Intimacy was recovered, because both were willing to seek change in the safe place of a counselor's office.

Life is hard. Relationships are messy. Careers are disappointing. Expectations are crushed and reality can be less than desirable. We MUST establish a place of refuge with the Lord. Time alone with Him gives us rest from the 'fight.' I've wrestled with God in quiet times before and gotten up feeling recharged and ready to attack some areas of change with His guidance and wisdom. I've also entered into mornings of quiet study with Him and left our time feeling more lost and confused than I was at the start. Either way, time alone with my Father has always given me a focus for the day. He alone knows what's coming our way, so He should be the One to direct our steps.

This morning, I sat down to type just about the time I should have been leaving for the gym. My writing schedule has been interrupted due to other things pulling at my time this week, so I felt it would be appropriate to skip the gym and write instead. A few minutes later, I hit a writing wall *again* and felt the leading to go on to my class. With boxing gloves on, sweat running everywhere sweat can run, and my lungs gasping for air, I heard the trainer use a phrase I believe I was supposed to hear today. He had given us a break to step away from the punching bag and he said, "before you come back and throw the first punch, make sure you're ready to fight again!"

Since this life is a battle, shouldn't we establish a daily time for breaks? We need the safety of a time-out. Intentional or unintentional, sin sidetracks callings and hinders reaching our goals. We are on the move with God, so we should give Him our wounded places, our mess-ups, our confusion, and our disappointments *quickly*. Establish time to step back, catch your breath, and hear the wisdom of your Father. Throw the next "punch" when He has made you ready. Continue visiting that established place of refuge daily. If we're willing to change, it may not be the most comfortable place on the journey, but I'm positive it's the safest!

> *The name of the Lord is a strong tower;*
> *The righteous runs into it and is safe*
> (Proverbs 18:10).

Day 27:
Give!

⤫

Read Joshua 21

I t's hard to believe we are approaching the end of our month together in Joshua. I pray God's hand of guidance has instructed you each and every day. Your journey probably looks very different from mine. That's OK, because my journey looks different than Joshua's. Still, I believe the instructions God gave the Israelites through the pages of Joshua are applicable to our lives too. Just like them, we can choose to disobey, but that choice forfeits blessing. Do we want the difficulty of obedience that leads to abundance or the difficulty of disobedience that always ends in loss? We *do* get to choose!

I've been completely shocked at the number of times during this process God has asked me to write about a concept, a calling, or a command that I haven't fully figured out for myself yet. When I read books, I always assume the writer has mastered everything she has written about. Maybe that's the case for some authors, but it's not the case for me. I am fully convinced each of these commands are necessary for following God, and that He can be trusted with my obedience. However, I'm still on the journey. I have not arrived. There's no area where that reality is more obvious than the area of *giving*.

As I was reading through this chapter in Joshua, I kept wondering how willingly each of the tribes gave up their piece of territory to the Levites. Can you imagine? They had been traveling for years with no land to call their own. They'd moved across territories, fought battles, and made plans for the land that God would give them. Then, at the beginning of our reading today, the Levites approached Joshua for their portion. I can imagine it was difficult for some to part with land they'd waited so long to receive. It's very likely they panicked and worried they'd run out of land for their people *if* they handed over a portion to the Levites.

Isn't that where the struggle with giving always begins? Don't we somehow fear we will out-give God and then do without what we need to live? Giving our tithes and offerings provides a concrete way to demonstrate trust in God for our future. I believe we will remain physically, emotionally, and spiritually stuck in ruts of unbelief until we fully obey the command to give.

> *Bring the whole tithe into the storehouse, so that there may be food in My house, and test Me now in this, says the Lord of hosts, if I will not open for you the windows of heaven and pour out for you a blessing until it overflows* (Malachi 3:10).

Concerning our tithes and offerings, God says, "Test me in this." After years and years of struggling in the area of giving, I'm ready to do just that. Quite honestly, my own way has never worked, so I might as well test His. The reason I can imagine a few of the negative responses the Israelites may have had is because I've had them for myself. But, we are so ready to trust the Lord and follow His way fully that we are becoming less and less attached to our ways of living. I want to be a cheerful giver. Again, it's a process, but the Lord has given me permission to test His way. For me, that has turned into questioning.

- **What is the starting point?** I know that scripture is very clear about ten percent being our smallest tithe. If you're like me and tithing isn't natural, perfection in giving isn't going to be the first step. I've had to ask God to help me determine an amount that I can give to my church monthly. My responsibility is to write that check immediately after hearing His answer. I also have to be ready to obey when the percentage well exceeds 10%.

- **How do I move forward and *test* God in giving?** A starting point in giving is just the beginning. No race ends at the start line. The Holy Spirit is a very powerful communicator and will continue to instruct all the days of our lives. When I've been sincere in seeking a way to grow in giving to the Lord, He's faithfully guided me in making a plan to obey more fully. Last year, God instructed me to increase my monthly giving by a certain amount. It was an act of faith. But, when the Lord directs, we have to be willing to follow through quickly.

- **Can we have the conversation again?** Yes! By nature, I'm just a fearful person when it comes to making mistakes. I'm embarrassed to admit that there have been a lot of months that I chose not to give because I didn't know what to give. My uncertainty paralyzed me, so I gave nothing. When I heard a friend say that the conversation about giving can be an ongoing one, I felt such freedom to give and then wait for God to instruct. The offering plate passes weekly. The church office is open daily. Most of the time, online giving is available 24 hours a day. Therefore, God can ask for more sacrificial giving at any time. Fear has no place in the conversation.

As I said, I'm a work in progress in the area of giving, but I'm open to all God wants to do in my life as He teaches. It's been a little over a year since He and I started wrestling with tithe. I'm sad to say I wrote the first check hesitantly. Shortly after, God led me to increase my tithe check a little. At the end of the year, I sat in a business meeting in the worship center of our church. Business meetings are typically no fun, although this one was a blast! Committee chairmen and ministers shared budget information with JOY. For the first time in many years, our church was ahead in giving. We were extremely ahead in giving, actually. After a celebration, we all committed to pray for wisdom in determining what to do with the excess. What a problem to have!

I got in my car that night and cried, "Thank you!" That meeting wouldn't have been nearly as fun if I hadn't been a part of the giving. Now, my contribution was pretty small in comparison to the overage, but I participated and was determined to continue. I never want to miss out on giving to God's work in my church. We tested and God passed. Although our financial situation wasn't dramatically changed, our hearts were. In giving up control we thought we had over our finances, we are discovering that God is true to His Word. When He calls for obedience in the area of giving, there's joy and peace to be experienced by the giver.

Maybe you are way ahead of me in this area, and I'm very proud for you. You keep doing what you're doing. *Share your stories of God's faithfulness in your sacrificial giving with others.* Those stories are a blessing. I've been encouraged to obey God in tithing through the stories of cheerful givers. When you are obedient in giving, and God is faithful in blessing, tell someone about it. Your story could be used in a powerful way.

If you are where I was just last year, start the process. Begin by praying about what God would have you give. I wholeheartedly believe there are areas of abundance He will withhold until we give to His Church with open hands. None of it is ours and none of it is actually our security. He who *owns the cattle on a thousand hills* is the One who cares for you and me. Remember, He's given you permission to test Him on the matter.

> *Honor the Lord with your wealth and with the first fruits of all your produce; then your barns will be filled with plenty, and your vats will be bursting with wine* (Proverbs 3:9–10).

Day 28:
Witness in Relationships

Read Joshua 22

Relationships are such a *gift*. I'm grateful for the people God has given to encourage, support, love, and advise me in this life. At every stage and season, delightful and positive relationships have blessed me in powerful ways. I am the person I am today because of so many people that have invested in me.

Relationships are *hard*. Because we are sinful humans operating in a fallen world, our interactions with people—even people that we love—can be difficult. It doesn't matter what kind of relationship it is: family, friend, work, school, etc. People in our lives have the ability to confront all of our issues and push all of our 'buttons.' Relationships can be the greatest sin exposer.

Relationships are *good*. The beauty of the mess Scotty and I have walked through is that we've been forced to see benefit in all relational encounters. If our purpose after salvation is to become more like Christ and to lead others to Christ, relationships could possibly be our priority ministry. Both positive and negative relational interactions can serve to fulfill our calling here on Earth, because exposure is a necessary step towards sanctification. Sadly, I've noticed that very few people (even believers) are open to utilizing this process within relationships.

The story we read in Joshua may have been hard to follow. I'll admit, I read it several times before I could even determine what was going on and find the main idea. I'm still not one hundred percent I've found it. However, through the verses we read together today, I was struck with a relevant question for believers. Why can't we see the importance of honoring God in our relationships with others? We serve a relational God. Sending Jesus Christ to Earth for us was a relational decision. Yet, we are so quick to discard relationships, resist processes, and blow past lessons that we are missing out on personal growth and outreach opportunities.

In Joshua 23, the last of the tribes was leaving for their inheritance. This move would require them to cross back over the Jordan River to possess their land. On the way back, they built an altar by the water. When the other tribes heard of it, they had an interesting response:

> *And when the sons of Israel heard of it, the whole congregation of the sons of Israel gathered themselves at Shilon, to go up against them in war* (Joshua 22:12).

The other men of Israel *heard* about the altar. They *gathered up* an army of men and prepared to *war* against their brothers. They'd fought battles *together*. They'd trudged across the wilderness *together*. Against all odds, they crossed over to victory *together*. Yet, upon hearing an assumed negative report, fear created division.

Five years ago, Scotty and I landed on a giant sofa in the basement of a beautiful home in Branson, MO. We sat in that spot for a solid week talking with other couples and two therapists. Until that point, I was NOT a fan of discussing feelings and emotions. Before that week, I absolutely hated confrontational conversation. However, after experiencing a relationship blow up, talking was a must. Our therapists led us well.

During that week, we helped each other figure out how and why we respond in relationship as we do. Some of the people on those couches weren't open to growth. For those of us that wanted a better way to communicate, the teaching we received was LIFE. See, all of the yuck that lies within us is exposed by the people in our lives. Family, friends, and co-workers often serve as God's sandpaper to smooth out the rough edges. Sandpaper hurts and the process is messy, but the outcome is always a more refined product.

We left our week of intensive therapy with necessary tools to rebuild communication in our marriage. I honestly do not think we would have survived without that instruction. We continued therapy at home for quite a while. Through it, we found that we were entirely too quick to jump to conclusions in *all* of our relationships. It's simple to become irritated, blow up, and shove people and relationships to the side. It's much harder and requires much more maturity to expose the root of the problem and seek growth. That's God's process for sanctification. Every time I've allowed the filth that bubbles to the surface in a negative confrontation to send me to the feet of Jesus, He's taken it and replaced it with a little more of Himself.

As hard as it was for me to follow this chapter in Joshua, I'm so thankful I stuck with it. These two groups of Israelites were headed for war. Both sides were given an opportunity to share their feelings. One side *feared* their brothers were sinning by building an inappropriate altar. That act would have been worthy of war. Our study of Achan is evidence that we must not deal lightly with sin in the camp. Then, the other side had the opportunity to share:

> *The Mighty One, God, the LORD, the Mighty One, God, the LORD! He knows, and may Israel itself know. If it was in rebellion, or if in an unlawful act against the LORD do not Thou save us this day! If we have built us an altar to turn away from following the LORD or if to offer a burnt offering or grain offering on it, or if to offer sacrifices of peace offerings on it, may the LORD Himself require it* (Joshua 22:22–23).

Do you see it? There was a misunderstanding. God's chosen people were headed into battle *against themselves* over a misunderstanding. Y'all, we do it all the time! As believers, we are God's family. We are brothers and sisters joined by the blood of Christ and the ministry of the Church, yet we bicker, fight, and war over misunderstandings.

The Israelites in Joshua did the ONLY thing that should be done in times of misunderstanding between God's people. They placed God, The Mighty One, the LORD, in the center of the dissension. Both sides of the argument were willing to let God be judge by seeking Him right in the middle of the dissension.

Why don't we get to witness more of God's people being willing to step back and allow God to judge?

May I gently suggest that our pride and arrogance may be getting in the way? The humility of the Israelites is amazing to me, because they weren't afraid to be wrong. After several years of sitting in a therapist's office, I'm no longer afraid of being wrong. On more than one occasion, I've been confronted with mistakes, failures, and faulty beliefs. I'm so thankful for those times because exposure allowed removal. I'd rather suffer some humiliation and grow in the sanctifying process the Lord has for me, because the other option leaves me *unchanged*. I can't think of anything worse than waking up tomorrow exactly like I am today. I could just go on to Heaven if that was the plan, but I'm still here. There's growing, maturing, and transforming to be done.

Now, don't get me wrong. I don't always *like* the process. It's painful. Sometimes, it's embarrassing. Most of the time, it's infuriating. It's always worth it, though. Do you know what I've realized? The people in my life that I admire most are those that welcome the difficult conversations. Leaders that gain my respect are those that aren't threatened when others have a different opinion. I love to see ministries that are able to come together with differing views because they share the commonality of God, the LORD, The Mighty One at the center of their relationship.

Oh it's a rarity, but when it happens, people watch! Unity among believers catches the attention of the world. We are so eager to be the change, to do the thing, to be part of the BIG ministry when the greatest WITNESS we could have is to unite with our brothers and sisters. If we could swallow our pride long enough to look to our Father, I believe He'd remind us that He sent His son to die for *relationship.* Salvation is gifted in *relationship.* So, the part of me that refuses the grace of salvation *in relationship* must DIE so others can witness the Gospel story.

Listen, I've confessed I'm lacking a theological degree. This is not a test and I feel comfortable in offering you the lessons God has taught me in this scripture. The Israelites gave the altar a name. The place where they came together in disagreement and departed in unity was called WITNESS. I don't know if it meant the same thing for them as it does for me. However, I'm positive that as long as we live, Scotty and I will never have the opportunity to be the WITNESS of God's Gospel story like we were at the point where we chose to make our marriage the altar of unity rather than division.

Our Joshua journey is almost over, friends. I can see the end. Where are you during this season of your life? When is the last time you allowed God to change you in a disagreement? Our spiritual journeys are individual. God's work in our lives is personal, but He often chooses to accomplish His goals for our character within a relationship. Certain elements of our callings could be forfeited if we refuse the fullness of God's sanctifying work in our lives. Please, don't hold on to reactions, personality traits, and character flaws that don't bear witness to His Great Name. Humbly lay them down and move on in joy. Be a WITNESS to the Gospel's power in your relationships!

> *Therefore, if any man is in Christ, he is a new creature; the old things passed away; behold, new things have come. Now all these things are from God, who reconciled us to Himself through Christ, and gave us the ministry of reconciliation, namely, that God was in Christ reconciling the world to Himself, not counting their trespasses against them, and He has committed to us the word of reconciliation* (2 Corinthians 5:17–19).

Day 29:
Be Careful!

Read Joshua 23

Walking with Joshua from the wilderness into the Promised Land has been therapeutic for me, because the road has been similar to my own journey of healing. God used desert adversity to draw the Israelites to *Himself.* He couldn't allow them to enter the Promised Land until they were completely dependent on Him for life in it. God has done the same in me for the past five years by walking with me through pieces of pain, confusion, and hurt for the purpose of finding freedom's rest in Him. *That's hard but sanctifying work.* Honestly, I hope I never forget the painful process He and I have completed together. Psalm 34:18 says, *The LORD is near to the brokenhearted, and saves those who are crushed in spirit.* I want to remember my season of hurting because I found my Rescuer there.

Mainly, though, I want to remember the pain of this particular journey, because it serves as a reminder to *live carefully.* We've made mistakes and received consequences. Godly counsel has given us the opportunity to analyze our choices and responses. We've experienced *obstacles* in recovery. The entire process reminds me that I desperately *need* God. Scotty and I don't wish away a single negative experience, because each one has been used to teach us more about ourselves, our God, and our necessary dependence on Him. Our failures remind us to move forward with **caution.** *That's a holy reminder.*

However, if we land at this chapter of Joshua and reduce his caution to a list of things we can't do, can't watch, or can't say, I'm afraid we've missed the point. At the end of his life, I believe Joshua was warning against religion as much as immorality. When I read this chapter, I hear a pleading to live boldly and to stand guard against fearful safety. In the wilderness, Joshua and the people were forced to cling to God and follow him wherever He went. In the Promised Land, God's people needed to war against idolatry.

> *But you are to cling to the LORD your God,*
> *as you have done to this day.* (Joshua 23:8)

The irony of the Christian life is that we have to *know* our weakness in order to live with strength and that understanding can only be acquired through experience. My husband's failure in the areas of marriage and ministry was the outcome of a lifetime he'd lived in bondage to insecurity and self-hatred. His sin only exposed the sickness. God allowed an enormous failure to uncover a need. Scotty chose to receive his consequences with humility and use them to strengthen his relationship with Christ, his understanding of himself, and his calling as husband and father.

In Scotty's case, I'm not sure there was another road to freedom other than the initial path of bondage. The details of the story he had to confess five years ago were awful and the pain they caused was terrifying. But, the results have been amazing. I feel like I have been given a front row seat to a modern day miracle story. It's changed the way I pray for myself and the people I love.

Watching Scotty's story and transformation keeps me from praying for God to remove all sin, sickness, and negative life events. If God plans to use an undesirable event to transform hearts in a desirable way, I can't pray it away. Hard lessons produce conviction. Difficult experiences create disciplined living. While I sometimes want an easier life, I know simple doesn't build substance, which is what it will take to *live carefully* and hold freedom's ground.

Thankfully, God didn't call me only to watch Scotty's transformation. He called me to my own. From the outside, I'm sure it appeared that I gave up freedom to do the right thing and 'stand by my man.' It never felt like that, though. There were lessons He taught me that I couldn't have learned any other way. Prior to that point, legalism and rule following allowed me to create a fairly manageable life; true dependence on God hadn't been completely necessary. If I'd never experienced the pain of adultery, I would have missed the beauty of a rescue. My ways and plans had failed, but God never did.

Please don't miss the importance of Joshua's end of life speech to the Israelites. At first glance, it may sound like fear. If cautious living could be done independently, anxiety would be an appropriate response. Joshua's answer, though, required repeating what they'd learned to do in the wilderness, to *cling to the LORD.* That's relational living with an all-powerful God. Nothing is too difficult for Him. Without a connection to God through Jesus, *be careful* means to follow a set of rules which leads right back to bondage. When life hits hard and God performs a miracle in the mess, we learn that living carefully means relying fully. It's the only way to maintain freedom.

Be very careful, then, how you live—not as unwise but as wise, making the most of every opportunity, because the days are evil. Therefore do not be foolish, but understand what the Lord's will is (Ephesians 5:15–17).

Day 30:
Choose Your Master!

Read Joshua 24:1–28

Prior to our Joshua study, you may not have been familiar with too many verses in the book, but today's reading certainly included a verse we hear often. In fact, it's painted on a frame in the entryway of my home:

> ... *choose for yourselves today whom you will serve; whether the gods which your fathers served which were beyond the River, or the gods of the Amorites in whose land you are living; but as for me and my house, we will serve the LORD* (Joshua 24:15).

Why did Joshua have to tell the Israelites to choose whom they would serve? The one, true God led them across the Jordan where water literally stood in a heap. Were there really any other options? Their ancestors had lived in Egypt as slaves for 400 years where a multitude of gods were proven powerless against God's plagues. Was another test needed?

I've had a difficult time figuring out how to write today's devotional. Sadness and frustration color all of my thoughts because I *know* the Israelites don't choose to serve the Lord forever as they promised to do in Joshua 24. God drew His people out of slavery in Egypt and they are going to walk right back into captivity. It's maddening and could be scary without taking to heart that we were *created to be mastered.*

In his final speech to the Israelites, Joshua asked his people to look over all of the possibilities and choose who they'd serve. He presented two specific options, God and the foreign gods; the latter had apparently been traveling with God's people since Abraham left Ur. The wording he used tells me Joshua knew the message I believe God has taught me today.

Everyone is a slave. Joshua didn't stop with the command to put away the lesser gods. He instructed the Israelites to choose a different master. *We all have a master.*

> *Now, therefore, fear the LORD and serve Him in sincerity and truth, and put away the gods which your fathers **served** beyond the River and in Egypt, and **serve** the LORD* (Joshua 24:14).

Very early in our healing, Scotty was confronted with the truth that He'd been ruled by self-hatred and self-pity for many years. Those gods stood in direct opposition to God and spoke many lies. In listening, Scotty chose his master. He believed the deceit and chose the wrong god. For too many years, he lived in darkness and missed out on the beauty and joy of our growing family.

I've been confronted with the shocking revelation that I chose the wrong master, too. For most of my life, I remember having the dream of family. At ten years old,

I begged God to keep my family together. As a teenager, frustrated by the fact that separated parents and step-family issues made me different, my heart longed for the day when I would get to make choices for a family. When my tall, dark, and handsome guy *finally* looked my way with forever on his mind, I began to plan for the future I'd always wanted. During the season when parenting revealed we needed help to establish a home different than what we'd been taught, I chose image over intimacy and religion over relationship. My master was pride, and it ruled all of my choices.

My bondage looked different than Scotty's, athough it was still bondage. In many ways, it was even more dangerous. Scotty knew he was missing something. He felt miserable in his sin. Meanwhile, our family was growing. Our three beautiful children created the family I'd pictured so many years before. The atmosphere at home felt heavier and tenser than I'd imagined it would, but I prayed for contentment and probably sounded holy in doing so. My foreign gods, pride and image, encouraged me to settle for good without even considering that God might desire more than *good* for His children.

Thankfully, in the early moments after Scotty's confession, Almighty God destroyed the idols of pride and image in my heart. Humility rushed in and the veil was removed. I saw life more clearly than I'd ever seen it before and I wanted God's best instead of His good no matter the cost. Honestly, that was my miracle because I know I wasn't prepared to choose well in those first moments.

Now, I have to *continue* choosing best. Every single day, I must make the choice to surrender my will for His. I want more than *the image* of a loving home; I want the real thing. So, I put away the foreign god, pride, and replace it with God and His Word. I choose to serve the One that established family and can use the good, bad, and ugly to create it in us.

> *No one can serve two masters; for either*
> *he will hate the one and love the other, or*
> *he will hold to one and despise the other*
> (Matthew 6:24).

It's very possible I was in even more danger than Scotty prior to 2011. I was serving the wrong gods, but they were respectable. Honestly, I was pretty happy with my *good* life. Pride, religion, law, and a positive image brought complements and made life feel quite manageable. God showed me more, though. I don't ever want to go back. Pride and image are terrible gods, and I must put them away. Then, I have to replace them with God. I was created for slavery. I just get to choose my Master.

You do, too! In complete humility, I'm asking you to examine your heart and determine your master. All of us are controlled by fear or faith, religion or relationship, gods or God. One leads to death. The other leads to fullness of life. You must choose, because freedom is at stake. Please don't settle for *good* when *best* is the offer.

> *Do you not know that when you present your-*
> *selves to someone as slaves for obedience you*
> *are slaves of the one whom you obey, either*
> *of sin resulting in death or of obedience*
> *resulting in righteousness?* (Romans 6:16)

Day 31:
Bury the Bones!

Read Joshua 24:29–33.

I suppose it's fitting that we end our journey together with a funeral. Joshua led his people well and died at 110 years old. Honestly, I'm experiencing graveside emotions as I write. It's hard to believe we are finished. We've arrived at our final destination. I don't know about you, but I have mixed emotions.

This morning, I was talking with the Lord and asking HOW to wrap this up. I'm just not ready! I believe He took me back to a song that literally *moved* me to begin this writing process. Scotty and I listen to Pastor Steven Furtick of Elevation Church weekly. His passion for Jesus is contagious and he has faithfully preached Truth; God has used it to bring us out of darkness and into light over the past three years. Elevation Worship released a new CD at the exact time God began urging me to write. In it, Pastor Steven spoke a powerful message within one of the songs. The title, "Move!," came from his words:

What happens on the mountain, can't stay on the mountain. What happens here has to get there. And, God's delivery system is faith.
There are some things in our lives, in our communities, and in our cities that, by the power of the Word of God and by the power of our worship are about to MOVE from here to there! Do you believe it?

I want to set an atmosphere and we want to see some things MOVE tonight in the presence of God. How many of you are ready to make a MOVE?
We're moving! We're moving from death to life! From darkness to light! From defeat to victory! We're crossing over from shame to grace, tonight! Somebody is moving from fear to faith! Somebody is moving from sorrow to joy, tonight!

We can't stay here. We've got to go. We have a charge to keep. We have a God to serve. We have a Gospel to preach. We aren't waiting on a MOVE of God. We are a MOVE of God.

Steven Furtick
"Evidence," *Here As In Heaven, 2016*

See, life is full of difficulties. It can be cruel, unjust, and downright mean. Like Joshua and the Israelites, everyone experiences seasons of difficulty. In those times, God often shows up and acts profoundly! He demonstrates His great power and we learn to depend on Him more fully. I don't believe God hides from us when life is pleasant, but I do believe we aren't as desperate in seeking Him. In the desert, awareness of God and His grace is heightened. So, to paraphrase Pastor Steven's words, *what happens in the desert can't stay in the desert! What's happened here (throughout the pages of this book) has to get there. And, God's delivery system will always be faith.*

The book of Joshua ended with a graveside service for Joseph's bones. Does anyone else wonder where those bones had been? Who carried them around? Please think about it, because Joseph's bones had *moved.* The Israelites had carried them across the Red Sea and the Jordan River. Bones traveled with the tabernacle and the Ark of the Covenant through the desert. It is likely Joseph's bones circled Jericho for seven days and waited securely through many battles in the Promised Land. Do you know why the Israelites carried them? Joseph told them to:

> *Then, Joseph made the sons of Israel swear, saying, "God will surely take care of you, and you shall carry my bones up from here."* (Genesis 50:25)

According to the message of Genesis 50, Joseph trusted two things: God would use the horror of slavery for His salvation story *and* God's children would not remain in bondage forever. He had no certain proof of either, but he believed God would act in the future as He had in the past. Joseph demonstrated great faith by asking that his bones be carried into freedom. Honoring Joseph's request, though, meant a visible reminder of slavery would accompany God's people to freedom. Then, in Joshua, it was time for the reminder to be buried.

There comes a time when we, too, must *bury the bones* of hurtful past memories, failures, and regrets. Cooperate with God and use the memories for healing and restorative purposes. Then, the pain must die and new direction and purpose are born. I've noticed that the lessons of the wilderness are never lost. The beauty of Joseph's life wasn't buried with his bones. I know that because Joseph's belief instructed me thousands of generations after he lived. Shortly after Scotty's confession, God brought to my mind Joseph's words in Genesis 50:20, *You meant evil against me, but God meant it for good in order to bring about this present result, to preserve many people alive.*

The bones of Joseph's life were buried, but the beauty of his faith lived on. Every time God's children choose to trust God's sovereignty in the darkest circumstances, Joseph's legacy lives. That gift made it all the way to me. I still remember quoting Joseph's words with confidence but without certainty. Today, five short years later, I've seen God do it. I can say to the Enemy,

You thought you'd won.

You were sure you'd destroyed another family and killed another witness.

But, my God was stronger and your mischief only showcased His miracles.

I get to bury the pain of adultery and walk away with a purified marriage and an enlarged faith. Praise God alone!

So, carry the bones until their reminders have driven you to the feet of Jesus where He delivers restoration and redemption. Plunder the Enemy and take back what he temporarily stole. Then, bury those bones, sister. Grab a memorial stone and mark this important date, friend. Because, *now,* it's time to *MOVE!*

> *The thief comes only to steal, kill, and destroy. I came that they might have life and might have it abundantly* (John 10:10).

CPSIA information can be obtained
at www.ICGtesting.com
Printed in the USA
FFOW05n1921131216